The Illustrated Book of
Table Games

The Illustrated Book of
Table Games

General Editor
Peter Arnold

Hamlyn
London · New York
Sydney · Toronto

The publishers wish to acknowledge with thanks
the assistance given by:
Harrods Limited of Knightsbridge, who loaned the
games equipment photographed on the jacket
Waddingtons Playing Card Co Ltd, for supplying
the playing cards used in the illustrations

Illustrations by Karel Feuerstein

Published by
The Hamlyn Publishing Group Limited
London · New York · Sydney · Toronto
Astronaut House, Feltham, Middlesex, England

Copyright © The Hamlyn Publishing Group Limited 1975

ISBN 0 600 34870 9

Filmset by Filmtype Services Limited, Scarborough
Printed in England by Chapel River Press Limited,
Andover, Hampshire

Contents

Contributors

PAUL LANGFIELD, who has written the *Chess* and *Draughts* articles, is engaged in educational publishing, and his interest in modern methods of teaching children has led him to write two books of chess instruction for them as well as a best-selling adult introduction to the game.

JEREMY FLINT is an internationally known bridge player, being a European Champion, an American Life Master and deviser of the Flint convention. He is also well-known as a leading backgammon player and has written the *Backgammon* article.

FRANCIS ROADS, who has written the *Go* article, is President of the British Go Association and an advocate of the game in magazine articles and on television.

RODNEY HEADINGTON is a contributor to magazines on games, and has written the article on *Hex*.

DAVID PRITCHARD is an authority on indoor games, as a writer and radio and television broadcaster. An international chess-player, he has written books on chess and go, and has edited books on other games. He is editor of the monthly games magazine *Games & Puzzles*. He has contributed the articles on *Reversi*, *Wari*, *Mah Jong* and *Dominoes*.

GEORGE HERVEY has written all the *Card Games* articles. A journalist, he began writing books and articles on bridge and other card games fifty years ago, and is currently bridge correspondent of *The Field* and the *Western Morning News*, posts he has held for 35 and 22 years respectively. He is author of, among other books, *The Hamlyn Illustrated Book of Card Games*, and as the recognised doyen of writers on card games is regularly consulted about the more obscure games.

PETER ARNOLD has written the articles on the gambling games, *Roulette* and *Craps*. He works for a publisher, and has edited many books on games and is author of *The Book of Gambling*.

Introduction

The recent popularity of backgammon, an ancient game, has emphasised what many people have known for a long time – that among the old-established games are some of the best, which will well repay learning. Many of the recent converts to backgammon will no doubt have begun a life-long addiction for the game. Go, similarly of ancient origin, and very popular in the East (there are about 500 *professional* players in Japan and Korea) has shown signs of increasing popularity in the West, and may well itself enjoy a similar boom.

Several such games are collected in this book. A player who learns to play some of them well will find that he will not easily discard them. The object is to describe in a clear way, with the help of many illustrative examples, how to play these games, and to give pointers on strategy, so that a learner will think about tactics along well-tried lines.

The book is divided into three sections. In the first, Board and Tile Games, will be found first a description of chess. There are sections on the openings, the middle game and the end game, and an instructive glossary of chess terms. Draughts is also described, with interesting variations on the basic game. Backgammon and go follow, each article running through a specimen game to help the learner. Hex, reversi, mah jong, wari and various domino games complete the section. All are games of skill, most have been proved by time (wari has been played in Africa for several hundred years), and all have a fascination hard to resist.

The second section deals with card games, and includes a variety of the best. Bridge, of course, has pride of place. However, poker, which is included, has a quite different fascination, and if only two players are available, bezique, pinocle, piquet and gin rummy all have their addicts to claim that they are the best. All are described here. Nor is the solitary player forgotten – five of the best one and two-pack patiences are described.

The third section includes two gambling games, roulette and craps, which are included because they will be of interest to games players in their own right, and also because they are ideally suited to a discussion of odds and chances, which are a vital part of serious games playing.

It is hoped that readers will improve their play at the games they already know, and will learn a few new ones to give them life-long pleasure.

P.A.

oard and Tile Games

Chess, Draughts–Paul Langfield
Backgammon–Jeremy Flint
Go–Francis Roads
Hex–Rodney Headington
Reversi, Wari, Mah Jong, Dominoes–David Pritchard

Chess

The game of chess as played today has an interesting if somewhat obsure history. Originally evolved as a game for four players, various changes have taken place over a period of many centuries and it is generally agreed by modern players that the game as played today can hardly be improved upon.

Most authorities attribute invention of the game to the Hindus but no precise date can be given. It was probably devised during the fifth century A.D. and during the next hundred years spread from India to Persia. In the course of time it reached North Africa, Italy, Spain and by the tenth century most of Europe. England has the Norman Conquest to thank for the introduction of the game and the earliest chess book to be published here was Caxton's *The Game and Playe of the Chesse* which is dated 1474.

Originally called *Chaturanga* the pieces used represented the four divisions of an Indian army—elephants, mounted horsemen, horse-drawn chariots and footsoldiers. Originally the game was played with a dice which decided the piece a player should move. In course of time this was dropped and it was generally agreed that the player must decide which piece had best be moved to effect a Checkmate.

A number of changes have taken place during the centuries that the game has been played. The Queen was once a male figure in the shape of some sort of minister or adviser to the King. When chess reached the European Continent this piece became a Queen and much greater powers were conferred upon her. Whereas the male adviser to the King was limited to one square at a move the newly crowned Queen was granted the sweeping powers of both Bishop and Rook. This piece could now move across the board as far as the player wished using ranks, files or diagonals.

The rook has had many different shapes and forms in the past. Sometimes a chariot, sometimes an elephant, it is today represented as a castle turret. Bishops too have had changes of form and power. Once an elephant, the piece became a Bishop when chess reached England. In France however the change was to that of a court jester and the piece became 'le fou'.

Knights seem always to have been associated with cavalry and today the piece is represented by a horse's head. When Nathaniel Cook designed the pieces most of us play with today he persuaded his friend the eminent chess player Howard Staunton to allow the set to be named after him. The Knight in the Staunton set is a horse's head said to have been based on the famous Elgin marbles.

Pawns were foot soldiers in the original game and they appear as such in many chess sets today. The Staunton pieces represent the Pawn as a small ball on a bell-shaped base.

When learning to play chess it is best to use Staunton pieces because these are now used in chess clubs and at all chess tournaments throughout the world.

The Board and the Pieces

Chess is played on a board of 64 squares of which 32 are White and 32 are Black. It is very important that players ensure that the board is the right way round before they set up the pieces. Each player should have a White square at his right hand corner.

The squares are coloured light and dark–usually White and Black but sometimes Cream and Brown or even White and Green. They are not identified by letters or numbers except in theory. To be able to record games both letters and numbers have been given to the squares and the item on notation explains the two main systems. It is possible to play the game without knowing either of them but a player wishing to improve his play would do well to master both because not all books use the same system.

Object of the Game

The object of the game is for a player to defeat his opponent by capturing his King. In fact the King is not removed from the board, but as soon as he is manoeuvred into a position from which he cannot escape, the game is over and the player who has made the capture has won.

Players move alternately and, except when making a special move called 'castling' which will be explained later, only one piece is moved at a time. A piece can be moved to a vacant square or to one occupied by a hostile piece which is then removed from the board in this same move.

The player who has the White pieces has a slight advantage and decision as to who plays White is decided by lottery. It is usual for one of the players to hold a Pawn of each colour in his closed hands and for his opponent to point to or touch one of the hands. Whichever colour he has selected he plays in the first game and thereafter the players alternate.

Value of the Pieces

The rules of chess decree that not all pieces move in the same way and therefore some pieces are stronger than others. A player should know the value of the pieces he is using or he will very soon find that, even if he knows the moves and can play a game, he will have difficulty in winning.

You need not remember the following points which experts have agreed should be awarded to the pieces, but you should be able to list the pieces in your mind in descending order of value. Here are the values:

Queen   9 points
Rook   5 points
Bishop   3 points
Knight   3 points
Pawn   1 point
King   ?

Clearly the Queen is your strongest piece and then come your Rooks. If your opponent has a Queen and King left on the board at the end of the game, and you have two Rooks and a King, then theoretically you have the edge on him—by one point.

Bishops and Knights come next and are equal in value in the early part of the game but the position of pieces in the end game may give the advantage to one or the other of these pieces.

Pawns have the least value but players should not underestimate them. After all each one qualifies for exchange to a Queen if they can reach the opponent's back row! Furthermore a well positioned Pawn in the end game may tip the scales to victory for a player.

It is not really possible to give a reliable point value to a King. He is not a powerful piece but he is valuable. If you lose your Queen you can still play on. Lose your King and you lose the game!

Check and Checkmate
Your opponent's King is said to be in Check if, having made a move you find you are able to capture the King in your next move. It is required that the player say 'Check' so that his opponent is aware that some action must be taken to save the threatened King. If a player finds that his King is in Check and that there is no way of saving the King then that is Checkmate and the game is over.

The Figures
The figures in this article have been designed to show the movements of the various pieces and, for simplicity, only those pieces involved in the move with the hostile King are shown. In a game of chess there would probably be many more pieces on the board but

it was thought that these, if shown, would only confuse or distract the reader.

Notation

There are two different ways of recording chess games and it will repay the reader to master both. Neither is difficult to learn and once the shorthand is understood a player can record his own games and, just as important, play out on his own board the games played and recorded by the experts.

The system in common use in the English speaking countries is known as Descriptive Notation (or English Notation) but most other countries use what is called Algebraic Notation.

Descriptive Notation

A very simple code is used to designate the pieces. Each is referred to by its initials as follows:

King–K
Queen–Q
King's Bishop–KB
Queen's Bishop–QB
King's Knight–KKt or KN
Queen's Knight–QKt or QN
King's Rook–KR
Queen's Rook–QR

The Pawns are named after the piece they stand before, thus:

King Pawn–KP
Queen Pawn–QP
King's Bishop Pawn–KBP
Queen's Bishop Pawn–QBP
King's Knight Pawn–KKtP or KNP
Queen's Knight Pawn–QKtP or QNP
King's Rook Pawn–KRP
Queen's Rook Pawn–QRP

Now for the board. Each square has a number for White and a number for Black. White's squares are numbered from the bottom of the board on all illustration figures and Black's from the top. The numbers run from 1 to 8 in each file and the files are identified by the names of the pieces which occupy them at the start of a game. Hence you get K1 and Q1 in the centre of the back rank and K1 goes to K8 up the board for White. K1 for Black runs down the board to K8. The same applies to all the other files.

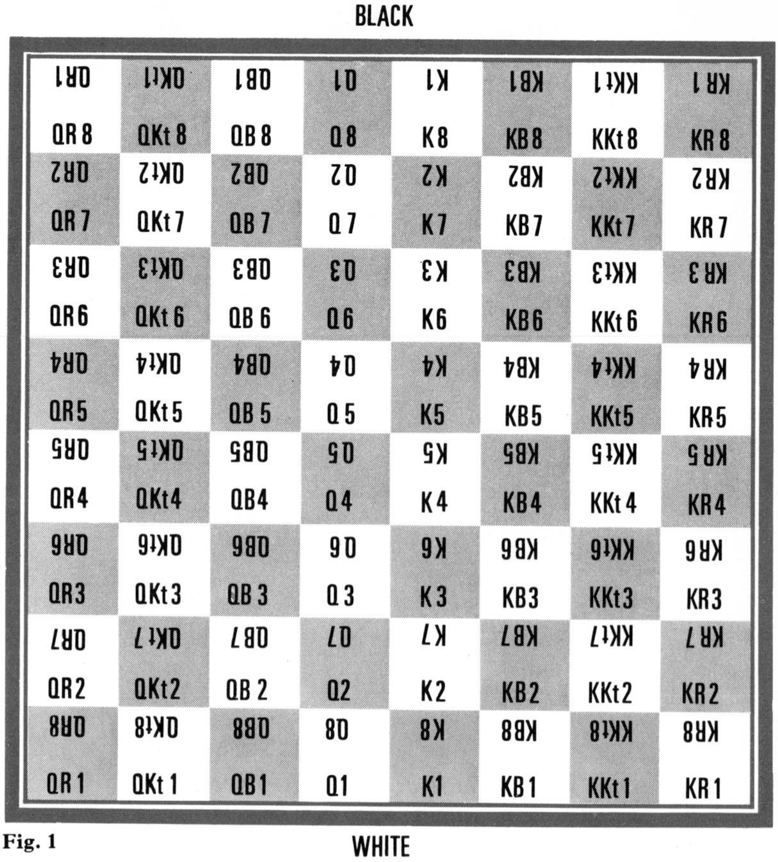

BLACK

Fig. 1   WHITE

Figure 1 shows the numbering for both White and Black. When recording movements always use the minimum shorthand. For example, if White's King Pawn opens the game by moving two squares forward this is written as P–K4. There is no point in identifying the Pawn as KP because it is the only one that can move to this square at this stage of the game. The dash (–) indicates 'moves to'. Other shorthand you should know is equally simple. The letter x = captures.

Therefore P x P simply means Pawn takes Pawn and this would apply if there is only one Pawn that can take another. If two Pawns have the option of capturing a hostile Pawn the one making the move should be identified such as BP x P (Bishop Pawn captures Pawn) or QP x P (Queen Pawn captures Pawn).

There are a few other simple symbols you should know about. Any move by any piece which puts the hostile King in jeopardy – that is to say a move which means that the King could be captured in the next move – is one that puts the King in Check. The player who has made this move must announce this by saying Check. It is recorded as simply ch after the move (example Q–R8 ch. The Queen has been placed in the eighth rank and in her next move could capture the King).

The move known as castling which will be fully explained later is recorded as O.O if made on the King's side of the board and O.O.O if on the Queen's side. The only other shorthand you need to know is the ! normally put after a good move by an analyst (example

14

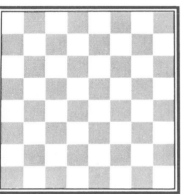

a b c d e f g h

Fig. 2

QxR ch ! which simply means Queen captures Rook and puts the King in Check, a good move) and ? which implies a move of doubtful worth, or a bad one. Sometimes one gets a combination of these last two such as RxB !? which means Rook captures Bishop—a daring move of doubtful wisdom depending on further moves by both players.

Algebraic Notation

Many players and especially chess writers prefer this system which is popular on the Continent. There is much to be said in its favour but, until it is more widely used in the English speaking countries, the reader would do well to master Descriptive Notation.

Algebraic Notation is easy to follow. The board is (in theory but not in practice) numbered from 1 to 8 up the files and from a to h across the ranks as shown in Figure 2. The history of this system goes back to Medieval times and was reintroduced about the middle of the 18th century.

The pieces with the exception of the Pawns are represented by their initials as in Descriptive Notation. The eight files have the letters a to h. The eight ranks have the numbers 1 to 8 starting from White's first rank. Black's first rank therefore is No. 8. The squares are therefore identified by a combination of letter and number.

A move is written as the initial of the piece plus the identification of the square it leaves and the square to which it moves. As in Descriptive Notation the act of moving a piece is shown as a hyphen or dash. To capture is shown as x.

Descriptive Notation gives the Ruy Lopez opening as follows:

White	Black
1) P–K4	P–K4
2) Kt–KB3	Kt–QB3
3) B–Kt5	and so on

Algebraic Notation of these moves is as follows:

1) e2–e4	e7–e5
2) Kt–g3	Kt–c6
3) B–b5	and so on.

Very few chess books in the English language use Algebraic Notation so the reader may think it best to concentrate on Descriptive Notation first.

Kings

Each player has a King. He is not the most powerful piece on the

15

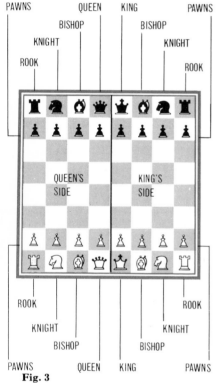

PAWNS QUEEN KING PAWNS
BISHOP   BISHOP
KNIGHT   KNIGHT
ROOK   ROOK

QUEEN'S   KING'S
SIDE   SIDE

ROOK   ROOK
KNIGHT   KNIGHT
BISHOP   BISHOP
PAWNS QUEEN KING PAWNS

Fig. 3

board but he is certainly the most valuable. This is explained by the fact that you may lose any other piece or pieces and carry on playing, but, if your King is captured, you lose the game.

Movement of the King is restricted to one square at a time except when making a special move known as castling which will be explained later. For the present, regard your King as valuable, slow moving and vulnerable. Take heart from the fact that this also applies to your opponent's King.

A King can use ranks, files or diagonals provided that he moves no further than one square in a move. Why should a player wish to move his King? The answer is that if a King is under attack and *can be taken* in the next move then the player under pressure must do one of four things. He must:

1) Move his King to a square which is not under attack – which explains why you might want to move him, or

2) the player must capture his opponent's attacking piece with his King. This he may not be able to do because the attacking piece may not be on a square adjacent to that of the King so he might

3) move another piece to place it between the attacking piece and the beseiged King. Alternatively the player whose King is attacked may be able to

4) remove the attacking piece with one of his other pieces.

If any of these moves can be made the game goes on. If not the King is Checkmated and the game is over.

Pawns

Each player has eight Pawns and these are placed directly in front of the other pieces as shown in Figure 3. For recording the movements of a game Pawns take the name of the piece they stand in front of and reading from left to right they are as follows: Queen's Rook Pawn (QRP), Queen's Knight Pawn (QKtP), Queen's Bishop Pawn (QBP), Queen's Pawn (QP), King's Pawn (KP), King's Bishop Pawn (KBP), King's Knight Pawn (KKtP) and King's Rook Pawn (KRP).

The rules governing Pawn movements are quite simple and apply to all Pawns. They always move forward and, except when making a capture, they always keep to the file in which they are placed at the beginning of the game. A Pawn is always moved one square at a time except in its first move when the player has the option of moving it two squares.

Pawns capture diagonally and this they can only do if there is a

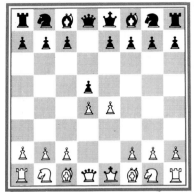

Fig. 4

Fig. 5

Fig. 6

hostile piece on the square ahead of them in the left or right adjacent file. Look at Figure 4. White has moved his Queen Pawn two squares forward as his first move and Black has replied with the same move P–Q4. The result is that both Pawns are blocked and can make no further move until one is captured and removed or makes a capture. Suppose that White now decides to move his King Pawn and to take advantage of the rule allowing a Pawn being moved for the first time to go forward two squares. Figure 5 shows his move P–K4. It is Black's move and because Pawns capture diagonally he takes White's Pawn as shown in Figure 6. If White had moved his King Pawn only one square it would not have been taken. Furthermore it would have been one square diagonally behind his Queen Pawn guarding it. In other words the King Pawn could capture any piece which took the Queen Pawn.

Pawns can capture any hostile piece in this way except the King but they can threaten the King. A Pawn can put a King in Check.

Promoting Pawns

There is one other very important thing you must know about Pawns. Although they are the least powerful pieces on the board, every one of them is a potential Queen. To achieve this promotion it is necessary for a player to get a Pawn to his opponent's back rank. This is never easy because there are so many hostile pieces waiting to attack any advancing Pawn. It is worth trying to achieve a second Queen because, as we shall shortly see, a Queen is more powerful than any of the other pieces and to have two on the board means almost certain victory. A strong player may well achieve this if playing against a beginner but good players of equal strength usually ensure that advancing Pawns are dealt with before they become eligible for promotion.

It should be mentioned that a Pawn reaching the eighth rank does not automatically become a Queen. The player can elect to exchange it for any other piece he cares to choose except, of course, a King.

Most sets of chessmen do not contain more than one Queen for each player so that if a Pawn is exchanged for a second Queen the player must improvise. If there is a Rook off the board at the time it is usual to use this with a Pawn balanced on top of it. More often than not a Pawn becomes a Queen late in the game when the player's Queen has been captured and is already off the board. She can now be taken back into service and is placed on the square which the successful Pawn reached.

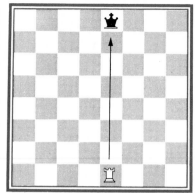

Fig. 7   Fig. 8   Fig. 9

Rooks

The movements which a Rook may make are very easy to learn. In a way it is the most straightforward piece on the board. A Rook can travel as far across the board as the player wishes provided that it is kept to a rank or a file. In other words the Rook can be moved forwards or backwards in a file or to the left or right in a rank. A Rook can put the hostile King in Check from the other side of the board. Look at Figure 7. The Black King is not in Check from the Rook because he cannot be captured in White's next move. Suppose White moves his Rook to the square shown in Figure 8 (R−K1). Now the Black King *is* in check and Black's next move must be to rescue his King. The arrow shows the path White Rook would take to capture the King.

Rooks can capture any hostile piece on the board by moving along the ranks or files and removing the piece from the square they travel to. Look at Figure 9. Black Rook can travel across the rank and capture White Bishop as shown by the arrow. If Black makes this move then White Pawn can capture Black Rook! This was a bad manoeuvre for Black because Rooks are more valuable than Bishops. This is where tactics come into chess. Only make a capture if it is really to your advantage to do so. Be sure you understand the relative values of the pieces and do not sacrifice a strong piece for the capture of a piece relatively weaker! If the protecting Pawn had not been in the position shown and the Bishop had been isolated, then the Rook capture would have been worthwhile.

Bishops

The movements which a Bishop is allowed to make are as simple as those of the Rook. The difference is simply that Bishops are confined entirely to the diagonals on the board. They move across the corners but never across ranks or up and down files. Like the Rook a Bishop can be moved as far as the player wishes provided that his path is unobstructed. Bishops capture by occupying the square of a hostile piece which is removed from the board.

One of your Bishops starts, and remains throughout the game, on a White square and the other on a Black square. This, of course, also applies to your opponent's Bishops.

As long as he is kept to diagonals a Bishop can advance or retreat provided the way is clear. When he takes a piece he occupies the square on which he made the capture and he remains on that square until moved again−or until he is captured.

18

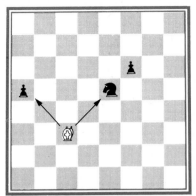
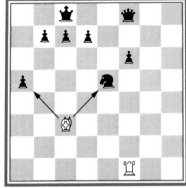

Fig. 10   **Fig. 11**

In Figure 10 the White Bishop is in a position to capture either the Black Knight or the Black Pawn. The Black Knight is protected by another Black Pawn so that if the Bishop does take the Knight he will be captured by Black Pawn. On the other hand if the player elects to capture the lone Black Pawn the Bishop is still safe. This would normally be the better move. It is a capture rather than an exchange.

In some circumstances an exchange would be the better move. In Figure 11 the White Bishop has the same choice of victims and elects to capture the Knight. If Black Pawn captures the Bishop the pathway is clear for White Rook to capture Black Queen and call Check. In fact, it is Checkmate because the Black King cannot escape from the back row. He is hemmed in by his own Pawns. White has made the sacrifice of a Bishop to win the game.

Knights

The movements of the pieces so far described have been simple to describe and should be easy to learn. The movement of a Knight does call for a little concentration because it is not quite so straightforward in its mode of progress across the board. A Knight moves two squares forward and one to the side every time it moves. It cannot elect to go one or two squares and then stop. It must make this L-shaped move or not move at all. Knights can advance or retreat and the movement across the squares can be two across a rank and one up a file or two up a file and one across a rank. Figure 12 shows a Knight moving out from its starting position and the arrow shows the square to which the player has elected to move it. Note

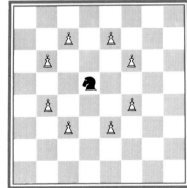

Fig. 12   **Fig. 13**

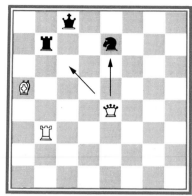 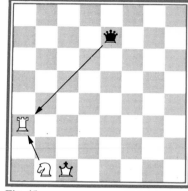

Fig. 14　　　　　　　　　　　　**Fig. 15**

that from this starting position there is one other square available to it and this is marked with a cross. Figure 13 shows a Black Knight in one of the centre squares. From this position the Knight can move to capture any one of the White Pawns round him. It should be remembered that Knights are the only pieces on the board which are allowed to hop over other pieces – and this applies to your own or those of your opponent.

Queens

Each player starts the game with a Queen. She is the most powerful piece on the board and the good player will ensure that, whatever move he makes throughout the game, his Queen is safe from capture. There are positions in which it may pay the player to sacrifice his Queen in order to ensure a Checkmate, but we will deal with this later.

Now for the movements a Queen is allowed to make. She combines the movements of both Rook and Bishop. That is to say a Queen may use ranks or files like a Rook or, if the player wishes she may use diagonals like a Bishop. She may be moved backwards or forwards across the board. Queens capture pieces in the same way as Bishops, Rooks or Knights. They occupy the square of the hostile piece and the latter is removed from the board. It should be mentioned that the Queen cannot make the Knight move. She is confined to ranks, files or diagonals.

In Figure 14 the White Queen is in a position to capture Black Rook or Black Knight as the arrows show. If the player elects to capture the Knight the game could go on with Black moving to get out of his difficulties. On the other hand if White Queen captures the Black Rook it is Checkmate. The Black Knight is not in a position to capture the White Queen and Black King cannot take her because if he did he would be moving into Check from the White Rook. The only escape square which might have been available to him is covered by the White Bishop.

If a Queen is in a position to make a capture always watch closely to ensure she does not put herself in jeopardy. In Figure 15 the Black Queen can capture White Rook and in the same move put White King in Check. Not a good move this because White Knight would then very promptly capture Black Queen! It is usually considered bad play to bring a Queen out into the open early in the game. She is powerful but like any other piece the Queen is vulnerable too.

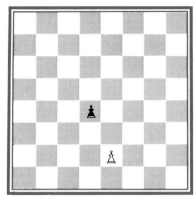 

Fig. 16   **Fig. 17**

Special Moves

There are two special moves a player should know about before he starts to play a game. The first of these is the En Passant move which is seldom made but nevertheless it should be understood perchance the player has the opportunity of making it.

En Passant

Stated briefly it is simply this. Any Pawn on the board when making its first move can go two squares forward but it cannot escape capture if it moves alongside a hostile Pawn. In Figure 16 White Pawn is about to be moved for the first time and there is a Black Pawn which in this position cannot capture White. If White takes advantage of the rule which allows him to go forward two squares then Black can capture White as if White had moved only one square. Figure 17 shows the move White Pawn has made and an arrow shows the square to which Black Pawn can now go and at the same time White Pawn is removed from the board. The result is a Pawn capture for Black as if White Pawn had moved forward only one square. The En Passant move does not crop up very often but the other special move does and the player should master it before starting to play. This is known as castling and it is usual for both players to make this move early in the game.

Castling

Each player is allowed to castle once during a game and experienced players usually aim to do it by about the tenth move – or soon after. In the one move the King is placed at the side of the back rank and a Rook is brought towards the centre of this rank. The object is to get the King to a place of greater safety and, at the same time, bring a powerful piece into active play towards the centre of the board. A player may castle on either side of the board depending on whether or not the way is clear for him to do so.

On the King's side the Bishop and the Knight must have vacated their squares before the player can castle. On the Queen's side the Queen herself must also have left her starting square. Figure 18 shows White ready to castle on the King's side and the arrows indicate the move about to be made. Note that after the move there is one White square at the corner. When castling is completed on the Queen's side there is both a White and Black square in the back rank corner. Figure 19 shows White ready to castle on the Queen's side (the arrows show the move). Figure 20 shows the move completed.

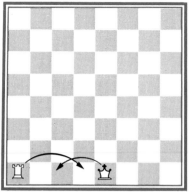

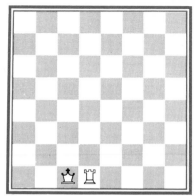

Fig. 18   Fig. 19   Fig. 20

A player cannot castle if his King is in Check, nor can he do so if either the King or the Rook have already made a move in the game. He cannot castle if the square he is to occupy or the one he crosses is under attack from a hostile piece. In other words he cannot move into or across 'Check'. The illustrations show the moves for the White pieces and exactly the same applies to the Black pieces.

Openings

There are many different ways of opening a game and a beginner would do well to study some of the well-known and well-tried variations. Games are named after the manner in which players use their pieces in the first few moves and have sometimes acquired the names from players who have introduced the opening or who were well-known for their use of it. Sometimes the place of origin gives its name to an opening and in some cases the name indicates the type of play expected. The Ruy Lopez opening is named after a sixteenth century Spanish priest who published an early textbook on the game and who was patronised by Philip II. The Spanish King invited Lopez to his court for games of chess. The Vienna Opening dates back to the Vienna Chess Congress of 1873 when it was used in tournament play and thereafter became popular with chess masters from Vienna. Examples of openings which anticipate the likely course of the game are Queen's Gambit Accepted and Queen's Gambit Declined. There are many variations on these openings and the beginner cannot be expected to master more than one or two openings to start with.

It is however worth studying the first few moves of some of the standard openings and some of these are given here.

Ruy Lopez

This is probably the most widely used opening of all. The moves start as follows:

White	Black
1) P–K4	P–K4
2) Kt–KB3	Kt–QB3
3) B–Kt5	

and depending on Black's third move the variations have additional titles such as Bird's Defence, Classical Defence and so on.

Examine carefully the first two moves for each player. White opens with a centre Pawn and Black replies with this same move P–K4 to stop the advance of White and give himself equality in the centre squares. White's second move Kt–KB3 is a threat to Black's Pawn and whereas Black could make a similar threat by copying White's move he in fact brings out his Queen's Knight. This is a defending move which shows White that Black will capture White's Knight if White dares to take the Pawn. Exchanging a Knight for a Pawn is a very poor move for White so he now goes B–Kt5. This is a threat to Black's Knight though the Knight is protected by two Pawns. If White Bishop captures Black Knight then Black Pawn takes White Bishop. Black's third move could be P–R3 (Morphy's Defence) which would drive the Bishop away or Kt–Q5 (Bird's Defence) which is an escape for the Knight and gives him a centre square.

For readers who would like to pursue further the Ruy Lopez opening here are some variations to try out.

Ruy Lopez   Classical Defence

	White	Black
	White	Black
1)	P–K4	P–K4
2)	Kt–KB3	Kt–QB3
3)	B–Kt5	B–B4
4)	P–B3	KKt–K2
5)	P–Q4	PxP
6)	PxP	B–Kt5 ch
7)	B–Q2	BxB ch
8)	QxB	P–Q4
9)	PxP	KtxP
10)	BxKt ch	PxB

The eleventh move could be for both players to castle. In terms of material captured, the players are equal. They both have more or less equal domination of the centre of the board. There is still room for development for both.

Ruy Lopez   Morphy Defence

	White	Black
	White	Black
1)	P–K4	P–K4
2)	Kt–KB3	Kt–QB3
3)	B–Kt5	P–QR3
4)	B–R4	Kt–B3
5)	O–O	KtxP
6)	P–Q4	P–QKt4
7)	B–Kt3	P–Q4

8) P x P   B–K3
9) Q–K2   Kt–B4
10) R–Q1   P–Kt5

This would follow on with (11) White B–K3, Black Kt x B and (12) RP x Kt for White. Here again the material captured gives equality to both players and domination of the centre squares is about equal. White has the advantage of having castled but the disadvantage of doubled Pawns in his Queen Knight file.

English Opening

This opening acquired its name because it was used on various occasions by the famous British nineteenth century player Howard Staunton. Its usual feature is that White opens with a Bishop Pawn leaving Black the opportunity to play for centre domination in the early moves. In theory White can counter this and by opening with a Bishop Pawn he is able to strengthen his position by quick development of his pieces. Here is one of the English openings:

English Opening Four Knights' Variation

White	Black
1) P–QB4	P–K4
2) Kt–QB3	Kt–KB3
3) Kt–B3	Kt–B3
4) P–Q4	P–K5
5) Kt–Q2	Kt x P
6) KKt x P	Kt x Kt
7) Kt x Kt	B–Kt5 ch
8) B–Q2	B x B ch
9) Q x B	Kt–K3

In the first nine moves each player has captured a Knight, a Bishop and a Pawn. Black has put White in Check twice and is already in a position to castle. Note that in the fourth move White offered a Pawn which Black refused and Black pressed on to threaten White's Knight. Having driven Black's Knight back, White must now continue development of his other pieces. It is anybody's game.

There are many other openings to study and readers who intend to take the game seriously should obtain a copy of one of the many books on chess openings.

Middle Game

This is the most difficult area to cover as far as instruction and

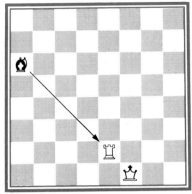

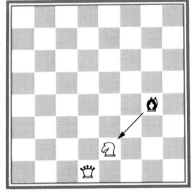

Fig. 21   Fig. 22

advice are concerned. There are so many different positions in which pieces may be placed on the board that it is only possible to give general guidance relating to a few common dangers to avoid. The beginner must always watch his Queen. Whatever move is contemplated he should look at it in the light of how does it leave his Queen when the move is made. He should also anticipate the next move of his opponent and make sure that, if it is an attack on the Queen, she can be saved before it is too late. This, of course, is in addition to safeguarding his King!

Pins

A piece which cannot or should not be moved is said to be pinned. Figure 21 shows a White Rook which is pinned by a Black Bishop. If White moved his Rook he would put his own King in Check which the rules do not allow. Figure 22 shows a White Knight pinned by a Black Bishop. If White moves his Knight, which he is allowed to do, he would lose his Queen to the Bishop.

A player who has a piece pinned should consider the following possible action:
1) capture the piece which is causing the pin.
2) move the piece which is being guarded to free the pinned piece.

Forks

If a piece is in a position from which it can capture either one of two pieces it is said to have them in a fork. Figure 23 shows a White Queen which in one move has put the Black King in Check and has forked Black Knight and Rook. When Black moves his King out of

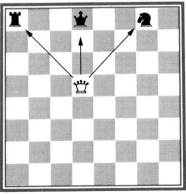

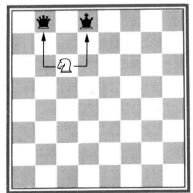

Fig. 23   Fig. 24

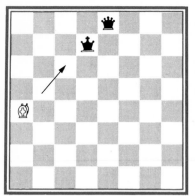

Fig. 25

Fig. 26

Fig. 27

Check White Queen can capture either the Knight or the Rook.

A particularly deadly fork is a Knight attack on King and Queen as shown in Figure 24. Black must move his King and then White captures Black's Queen.

Skewers

A skewer is an attack on one piece which, when moved to avoid capture leaves the attacker in a position to take another piece. In Figure 25 White Bishop has put Black King in Check. The King must move and then Bishop captures Black Queen. From this example it is clearly dangerous play to position your King in front of your Queen. Sometimes it is possible to force a King into this position. Figure 26 shows a Black Rook about to force the White King to move from the Rook file. Figure 27 shows that Black's second Rook can now Check Black King forcing it to move again so that Black Rook can capture White Queen. A skewer can take place on a diagonal, a rank or a file.

End Game

The final stages of a game offer opportunities to the beginner for worthwhile study. It is disappointing to capture material, avoid pins forks and skewers but fail to effect a Checkmate. Study the simple mates to start with. If a Queen can safely occupy a square adjacent to that of the hostile King when he is at the edge of the board then that is a certain mate. Figure 28 shows that White King is not in Check but it is Black's move. Figure 29 shows the winning move. White King cannot capture Black Queen because he would

Fig. 28

Fig. 29

Fig. 30

Fig. 31

Fig. 32

move into Check from the Bishop. There is no escape square to which he can now move.

A simple mate is often effected with two Rooks. The hostile King must be driven to the edge of the board. Figure 30 shows Black King in Check from one White Rook and he must move. The only rank available to him is the back rank because the second White Rook stops him coming forward. Figure 31 shows that he has retreated and now White moves his second Rook to the back rank and this is mate. Figure 32 shows the move.

It has been stressed that players should always keep a wary eye on their Queens to ensure that these are not captured. In the part dealing with Queen movements it was stated that in some positions a player may decide to sacrifice his Queen to ensure a Checkmate. Here is an example which is worth playing out on your board. The game has reached the 17th move (Figure 33). White goes P–QKt4 and Black brings a Bishop to call Check B–B7 ch. White must move his King. He cannot capture the Bishop with his King because this would put his King in Check from Black's Knight. White's move is K–QR1. Now comes Black's surprise move. He feels that his position is strong enough to risk his Queen and he goes Q–K8! (Figure 34).

Note that White could capture Black Queen now but his position is so desperate that he feels it is more important to get his King out of the blocked position it is in. He must make an escape route and to do so he moves P–R3. Black's next move is another surprise. It is KtxB! (Figure 35). There is nothing to stop White Rook capturing Black Queen now. This, of course, is what he does. Move

Fig. 33

Fig. 34

27

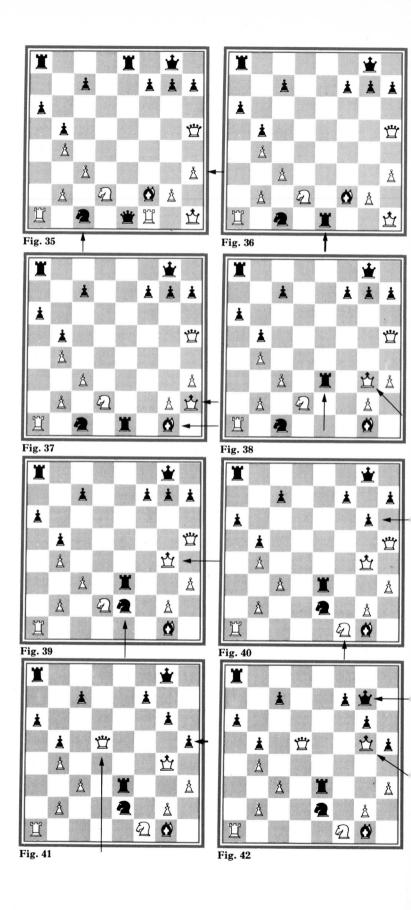

Fig. 35

Fig. 36

Fig. 37

Fig. 38

Fig. 39

Fig. 40

Fig. 41

Fig. 42

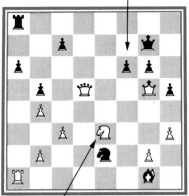

Fig. 43

Fig. 44

20 is R x Q for White. Black's reply is R x R ch! (Figure 36). White King is still on the run. He cannot capture the Rook so he must move. His foresight in moving out the Rook Pawn enables him to move K – R2. Black continues to press his relentless attack with B – KKt8 ch! (Figure 37). White King forlornly goes to KKt3 but Black hounds him with his Rook. The move for Black is R – K6 ch! (Figure 38). Once more the weary White King moves, this time to KKt4. This time Black does not put White King in Check but he rescues his Knight and brings it into the attack. His move is Kt – K7 (Figure 39).

White should really be concerned to rescue his King but he seems to hope for a distraction by threatening Black's Rook. He moves Kt – KB1. Black ignores this and continues to build up his attack on the King. This time he moves a Knight Pawn and threatens White's Queen, P–KKt3! (Figure 40). White saves his Queen by Q – Q5 and Black calls Check again with P – KR4! (Figure 41). White King goes to KKt5 and Black brings his own King into the fray. White's move is K – KKt5 and Black's K – KKt2 (Figure 42).

Because he is not actually in Check and because he aimed to do it a long time ago, White now captures Black's Rook. Black calls Check again by P – KB3 ch (Figure 43). If you put yourself in the position of the player with the White pieces you will see that White's next move is the only one open to him. He has to move his King and there is only one square available. There are five vacant squares of which four are under fire from Black pieces. So White moves K – KR4 and Black moves up his Bishop, B–KB7 ch! (Figure 44). Now comes White's last despairing move. It is P – KKt3 (Figure

Fig. 45

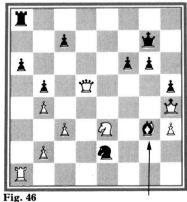

Fig. 46

Fig. 47

45). He is out of Check for only a matter of seconds. Black now captures this Pawn and calls Checkmate (Figure 46).

Study the position carefully. Black Bishop is Checking White King and it cannot be taken by any White piece. The King cannot capture it without moving into Check from Black Knight. The White Queen is on a wrong diagonal. White King cannot move to the only adjacent vacant square because this would be a move into Check from a Black Pawn!

For ten moves Black has managed without his Queen and in half of those moves he has been able to call Check.

In giving the value of pieces earlier in this article it was mentioned that although a Queen is the strongest piece on the board, a well positioned Pawn can tip the scales at the end of a game. This, indeed was just such a game!

And now to resignations, draws and stalemates. If either player is fairly sure that his opponent will soon effect a Checkmate and if he himself cannot possibly win he may well think it pointless to continue the game. He is therefore well-advised to resign and, of course, this means his opponent has won. On the other hand both players may find themselves without sufficient strength in pieces to effect a mate and it is usual for them to agree a draw.

On the other hand there is one form of draw which players with mating material on the board should strenuously avoid. This is stalemate. If it is your turn to move and the only moves open to you would mean exposing your King to Check when he is not already in Check, then that is a stalemate. You cannot move so you cannot win or lose. The result is therefore a draw. In Figure 47 the player with the White pieces cannot possibly win because he is reduced to a lone King. Black on the other hand has his Queen, a Rook, a Knight, a Bishop and a Pawn on an open file that might have become another Queen. But the result is a stalemate because it is White's move and he cannot move his King without moving into Check. Note that White is not in Check *before* his move. White therefore claims a draw.

Clearly this is a rather exaggerated position and Black has played very badly to allow this position to come about. To avoid a stalemate you must be sure that your opponent *can* move a piece without having to move his King into Check. You may hope for a stalemate if you are losing and your opponent is strong but it can only be a hope. There is no way of forcing your opponent to make the supreme blunder.

A Complete Game Analyzed

Here is a complete game with comments on the moves of both players. If you play this out on your own board you will find it easier to see whether or not you would have made the same moves.

Irregular Defence

White   Black
1) P–K4   P–K4

White makes a standard opening move with a Pawn placed in the centre of the board. Black's reply follows the convention of stopping the opening Pawn from going any further. Black also achieves equality in the game by occupying a centre square.

2) Kt–KB3   Kt–QB3

White brings out his King Knight. The position it now occupies is a threat to Black's King Pawn. Black's reply is bring out his Queen Knight to protect his Pawn. If White captures Black Pawn, Black would capture White Knight! Both players now have opening Pawns in the centre and each has a Knight ready for attack or defence.

3) B–B4   P–Q3

White advances his Bishop to a square from which it could take a Black Pawn (B x BP ch) and put the Black King in Check. This would be throwing the Bishop away if White makes it his next move because Black would reply with K x B. Losing a Bishop to take a Pawn is a poor exchange! On the other hand if White could in move 4 advance his King Knight to Kt5 he could *then* make the Bishop move with safety because the King would be unable to capture except by moving into Check which the rules do not allow. Black's reply is P–Q3. This move serves two purposes. Firstly it frees Black's Knight from its protective role guarding the King Pawn. Black's Queen Pawn now does this. Secondly it opens the diagonal for Black to bring out his Queen Bishop.

4) P–B3   B–Kt5

White's Pawn move is aimed at discouraging Black's Knight from advancing either to the centre (Kt–Q5) or to the Queen's side (Kt–Kt5). White's Pawn is ready to capture Black Knight if he jumps to either of these positions. White has also opened up another diagonal for his Queen.

Black's Bishop has now come out as we anticipated that it might. Black Bishop threatens White Knight but not very seriously because if B x Kt then P x B. But Black has pinned White Knight unless White is prepared to sacrifice his Queen. If White moves his King Knight then Black Bishop captures White Queen!

5) Q–Kt3 Q–Q2

White now takes advantage of the new diagonal for his Queen and goes to Kt3 on the same diagonal as his Bishop. Now if in his next move White Bishop captures Pawn it would be Check and Black King could not capture the Bishop because he would be moving into Check from White Queen.

Black can see this danger and moves his Queen one square so that, if necessary, she can capture Black Bishop if the Pawn is taken.

6) Kt–Kt5 Kt–R3

White is free to move the Knight that was pinned and he brings this up to support the attack he has mounted with his Queen and Bishop. The square under fire is KB7 for White or KB2 for Black. White now has two pieces either of which can capture the Black Pawn on this square. The White Bishop supports the Knight and White Queen supports the Bishop.

Black's reply to White's attack is to bring out his King Knight to a square from which it can capture any piece which dares to take the Pawn which is under threat.

7) BxP ch KtxB

Now comes White's attack. By taking the Black Bishop Pawn with his Bishop he puts the King in Check. As expected Black captures White Bishop with his Knight. White continues to press the attack.

8) KtxKt QxKt

In capturing Black's Knight with his own, White knows that Black King cannot be used against him because the King must not move into Check. If Black Queen takes White Knight there could then be an exchange of Queens. This is a risk Black is prepared to take and, though his King is not in Check he decides to capture White Knight with his Queen.

9) QxP K–Q2

White now switches his attack to the Queen's side of the board. Having failed in his attack on the Black King he elects to gain advantage in material by first of all snatching a Pawn. Black brings his King forward to Q2 to avoid Check if White now captures Black's Queen Rook.

10) QxR Q–QB5

Throughout the game so far White has done the attacking and Black has defended. In this tenth move the pattern starts to change. As expected White's new attack is aimed at gains in material and

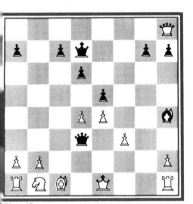

Fig. 48

capturing Black's Rook without loss appears good until you study Black's reply. The move to QB5 is the beginning of Black's winning attack. Study the position carefully. He already has a Bishop covering his K7 square and White has no escape paths open to him. He must start a brisk defence now or lose the game.

11) P–B3   BxP

White's Pawn move is a threat to Black's Bishop and halts the immediate attack but Black keeps the pressure on by capturing the Pawn even though he knows he must surely lose his Bishop. White must capture Black Bishop if he is to stay in the game.

12) PxB   Kt–Q5

White Pawn captures Black Bishop. In terms of material captured White is ahead but the pressure is on and Black's move Kt–Q5 is a further threat and at the same time a possible sacrifice. White should take the Knight with his Bishop Pawn.

13) P–Q3   QxQP

This is White's fatal mistake. By threatening Black's Queen with his Queen Pawn he had hoped to capture Black's Knight without loss. Black simply captures the threatening Pawn and waits for the kill. It is not far away.

14) PxKt   B–K2

So White now captures Black Knight. He is still gaining material but to little effect. Black's reply only tempts him to further indiscretion. By moving his Bishop from the back rank Black has exposed his Rook to danger from White's Queen. In fact this does not matter as the next move by both players clearly shows.

15) QxR   B–R5 mate!

White has fallen for the bait while Black has manoeuvred his Bishop into a winning position. White Queen captures Black Rook but Black Bishop moves to R5 and calls Check–in fact it is Checkmate (Figure 48). White has no piece to effectively intervene. White King is in Check and there is no escape square for him.

A short game this in which there are a number of noticeable features. Neither White nor Black castled in this game which is unusual for players of this stature. White did all the attacking in the earlier part of the game but Black's defence was always adequate. White gained more material but allowed himself to fall into fatal traps. Good aggressive play by White and brilliant cleverly calculated play by unruffled Black. The players were White Rodzynski and Black one of the really great chess players of all time, the legendary A. Alekhine.

Summary

Chess is not a game which is difficult to play nor is it really a difficult game to learn. There are, however, many rules to remember and a beginner should find the following At-a-glance A–Z useful when playing with an opponent who is also a beginner. A glance at the appropriate heading should lead to a quick answer to queries which may crop up in a game. There is also general chess information here.

At a Glance A–Z of Chess

Algebraic notation. This is a system of recording the moves in a game widely used on the continent but not much favoured in English-speaking countries.

The eight files are given the letters a to h from left to right for White and the ranks are numbered 1 to 8. The numbering starts from White's back rank. A move is recorded as the piece (not Pawns) identified by its initial and the combined letter-number of the square of departure and the square of arrival.

Back row. The back row is White's first rank and Black's first rank—that is the first line of squares running from left to right across the board and nearest to each player.

Bishops. Each player has two Bishops one of which is confined to White squares and the other to Black squares. All Bishops are confined to diagonals when they move but, provided the squares are unoccupied, they can move as many squares as they like in one direction. They can, of course change direction in the next move. Bishops capture by occupying the square of a hostile piece. They can put a King in Check if the diagonal from Bishop to King is unoccupied by White or Black pieces. One Bishop starts at the side of the King and the other at the side of the Queen. They are identified respectively as King's Bishop and Queen's Bishop.

Board. There are 64 squares on the board—32 White (or light coloured) and 32 Black (or dark coloured). When the pieces are set up for a game each player must have a White corner on the right of his back rank.

Capture. When any piece makes a capture it occupies the square of the hostile piece which is, in the same move, taken off the board.

This applies to all pieces from Pawns to Kings. A capture is indicated by a cross (x).

Castling. This special move is open to each player once in any game. The conditions governing the move are: The King must not have made a move before castling. The Rook must not have made a move before castling. The squares between King and Rook must be vacant. The King must not pass across a square under attack from a hostile piece. The King must not move into Check. The King must not be in Check. On the King's side the King moves two squares towards the corner of the board and the Rook two squares towards the centre and ends up therefore on the King's other side. To castle on the Queen's side of the board the King moves two squares towards the corner and the Rook three squares towards the centre of the board ending up on the King's other side.

Check. If a hostile King can be captured by a player in his next move then the King is in Check and it is customary for the player to say 'Check'. His opponent is obliged to get the King out of Check by moving the King to a safe square or capturing the attacking piece *or* placing a piece between the attacking piece and the King. The game can then proceed.

Check, discovered. If a player moves a piece which leaves the hostile King in Check from another piece then this is known as a Discovered Check.

Check, double. It is possible for a player to double Check the hostile King. An example is when a Bishop starts in front of a Rook which is in the file occupied by the King. The latter is not in Check but when the Bishop moves to a square of which the diagonal is in direct line to the King then there is a double Check – one from the Rook and the other from the Bishop. The King must escape from both.

Checkmate. If a King is put in Check and cannot escape from the Check, then that is Checkmate and the end of the game.

Chess clock. In tournament chess it is customary to decide before play begins how many moves a player must make within a given time. Special clocks are available with two faces and White's clock is started as soon as play commences. When he has made his move White presses a button to start Black's clock having stopped his own. Players keep a record of their moves and can see from their clocks how well they are keeping within the time limit for the game.

Descriptive notation. Sometimes called the English Notation because it is largely used in the English speaking countries, this is the method of recording games most likely to be of use to the reader. The files are identified by the initials of the pieces which occupy them at the beginning of the game. The ranks are numbered from 1 to 8 for both White and Black starting from the back rank of each. White's King square is K1 and this square, if Black reaches it is K8. In chess literature, White always plays from the bottom of the diagram. The pieces are identified by their initials and Pawns by P unless it is necessary to distinguish between two in which case they are further identified with the initials of the piece they stand in front of at the beginning of the game. A dash means 'moves to', and x means captures. Check is abbreviated to ch. (!) means a good move, (?) a bad move.

Diagonals. Moving across the diagonals of a board simply means moving across the corners. Bishops are confined to diagonals throughout the game. Queens have the option of using the diagonals as do the Kings though the latter, except when castling, are confined to moving only one square at a move.

Development. From the first move in the game each player endeavours to bring out his pieces to positions of advantage on the board. This is known as development. It can be impeded if a player's opponent gains an early advantage and plays an aggressive game. This inevitably means that defence and consolidation are called for and the player may be delayed in developing his pieces satisfactorily.

Draws. If neither player has sufficient strength to Checkmate it is customary for them to agree a draw. A draw can be requested by a player if the same position appears three times as a result of the same move being made by that player.

A draw can be claimed by either player if fifty moves have been made and no piece has been captured and no Pawn has been moved – an unlikely eventuality!

En passant rule. If a Pawn when making its first move advances two squares and avoids capture by drawing alongside a hostile Pawn then it can be captured as if it had moved only one square. The capturing move must be made immediately after the Pawn's two square advance and cannot be postponed until later in the game.

Forced move. This refers to the position a player finds himself in when the move he makes is the only possible move.

Exchange. When a player captures a hostile piece and then loses his own piece it is said to be an exchange. An exchange in which equivalent pieces are lost and won is an even exchange. An exchange in which a Knight or Bishop is captured for the loss of a Pawn is said to have been won – if the Pawn was captured in exchange for the Knight or Bishop the exchange is said to be lost.

Files. The rows of squares which run in line from your back row to your opponent's back row. In chess charts the files are the lines of vertical squares.

Files, open. An open file is one which is unoccupied by Pawns of either colour. Rooks do well in these.

En prise. A piece under attack and which is undefended is said to be *en prise.*

Fork. A fork is a double attack when a piece can, in its next move capture either one of two hostile pieces. To counteract a fork the player should consider a counter attack such as putting the hostile King in Check or capturing the piece responsible for the fork.

Gambit. A gambit usually means to offer a piece for possible positional advantage, and to enable the player making the offer to get early advantageous development. Some named chess openings have the word gambit in them such as Queen's Gambit Accepted or Queen's Gambit Declined.

Interpose. To interpose a piece is to place it between an attacking piece and the King to get the King out of Check. It also applies to relieving other pieces from attack such as placing a Pawn on a diagonal between an attacking Bishop and a Queen. The Bishop would then have to take the Pawn first and, if that square is safe, the Queen might then take the Bishop.

J'adoube. When a player has occasion to touch a piece in order to place it properly on its square and not to move it he should correctly say '*J'adoube*' or, more informally 'I adjust'.

Knights. These are the only pieces in chess which have the power to jump over other pieces (of either colour). The Knight's move is two squares in one direction and then one square in a different direction. He thus makes an L shaped move. The Knight can go two squares up a file and then one across a rank or two across the rank and one into the file. Knights can move forwards or backwards.

Kings. Kings are limited in their moves to one square in any one move except when castling takes place. The two Kings in a game must never be placed on adjacent squares. There must always be one square between them though this need not be vacant. King's can advance or retreat.

King's side. All squares on the right hand side of the board for White and left hand side for Black are referred to as the King's side.

Mate (see Checkmate).

Middle game. After the known moves of an opening and the final moves of the end game comes the major battle which is loosely referred to as the middle game. No precise number of moves constitutes either opening, middle game or end game.

Notation. The two most widely used systems of recording Chess games are Descriptive Notation (also known as English Notation) and Algebraic Notation. Both are described in this book.

Openings. The number of ways of playing the first ten moves of a game are some astronomical figure and the beginner cannot be expected to remember many of them, but he will remember a few as he becomes familiar with them.

Openings have been named after Master players with whom they have become associated, places or tournaments, or in some cases they have been named to indicate the likely course of play.

Pawns. The least powerful of the chess pieces, Pawns do have the chance of promotion if they can be safely taken to the opponent's back rank. The movement of the Pawn is one square forward in its own file except when it is moved for the first time when the player may, if he wishes, advance the Pawn two squares. Pawns capture diagonally and remain in the file on which the capture was made. Pawns never retreat and never hop over other pieces. Pawns can give check to a hostile King.

Pawn, blocked. A Pawn is said to be blocked if it can make no further progress forward because a hostile piece occupies the square immediately in front of it.

Pawns, doubled. When two Pawns of the same colour occupy the same file, as a result of a capture, the player finds he has Doubled Pawns. This impedes satisfactory play and development and should be avoided if possible. Doubled Pawns are weak Pawns.

Pawn, passed. A Pawn which has a clear run in its own file and no hostile Pawns on its adjacent files is known as a Passed Pawn.

Pieces. In this book, and many others, the term pieces refers to any of the chessmen including Pawns. Purists, however, limit the term to Queens, Rooks, Bishops and Knights. The Queens and Rooks are classified as major pieces and the Bishops and Knights as minor pieces.

Pin. A piece is said to be pinned if it cannot or should not move. A Bishop which stands in front of a King to stop a Check from a hostile Rook cannot be moved and is forcibly pinned. A Knight standing in front of a Queen is pinned if he prevents the Queen being captured. The player may have the right to move the Knight but would be well advised not to.

Promotion. When a Pawn reaches the end of its file (the 8th rank) it can be changed to any other stronger piece the player decides on. It is usual to choose a Queen. This is promotion.

Queens. Queens are the most powerful pieces on the board. This is because they can do more than other pieces. They can use ranks, files or diagonals and can move as many squares as the player chooses provided the way is clear, of course. They combine the powers of Rooks and Bishops. They are, like all other pieces, vulnerable and loss of a Queen is more often than not, loss of the game.

Queen's side. All squares on the left hand side of the board for White and right hand side for Black are referred to as the Queen's side.

Ranks. The lines of squares which run from left to right across the board are the ranks. In chess charts the ranks are the lines of horizontal squares.

Rooks. Second only to the Queen in power the Rooks are confined to ranks and files. They never move diagonally nor do they hop over other pieces. Rooks can travel as far as the player decides provided the squares are free and they capture by occupying the square of a hostile piece which is, in the same move, taken off the board.

Sacrifice. A player who allows a piece to be captured is said to make a sacrifice. This is done in the hope of obtaining an advantageous position which is not always obvious to the opponent.

Skewer. A skewer is an apparent attack on one piece whereas it is in fact an attempt by the player to capture a more valuable piece which is in the same line of squares but lying behind the piece attacked.

Stalemate. When a player can move no piece on the board except his King and if the King is not in Check but would move into Check if moved at all, then that is stalemate and the game is declared a draw.

Threat. If a piece can capture a hostile piece that is a threat.

Touched piece. If a player touches a piece the laws of chess decree that he must move it. An exception is when he is adjusting it on its square and this he must announce to his opponent (see *J'adoube*).

White, who plays? The decision as to which player has the White pieces is decided by lottery. It is usual for one or other of the players to conceal in each hand a Pawn of the two colours. His opponent then points to or touches one of the closed fists and plays whichever colour is revealed when the hand is opened.

Draughts

In Great Britain the game is called draughts and is played with Black and White pieces on a Black and White board. In the United States it is called checkers and the pieces are usually red and white and the board dark green and buff. The method of play is the same on both sides of the Atlantic though there are other variations such as Spanish draughts, German draughts, Russian draughts and Polish draughts. Other alternatives to the normal game are losing draughts and diagonal draughts.

The game is played on a board of 64 squares of which 32 are White (or light coloured) and 32 are Black (or dark coloured). Each of the two players has 12 pieces or men and these are round wooden or plastic discs coloured White (or light coloured) and Black (or dark coloured).

The discs are placed on the three rows of Black squares nearest to each player. Before setting out the pieces always ensure that the board is the correct way round by looking to make sure you have a White square in the right hand corner nearest to you (Figure 1). This is exactly the same as for Chess.

All play takes place on the Black squares and movement of the pieces is confined to moving forward on diagonals (across the corners of the squares). The pieces all have the same value and are all confined to the same type of move until they are advanced to the opponent's back row when they are crowned kings. This is done by placing a second disc on top of the successful one so that it is distinguished from the ordinary men. Kings can move in any direction on the diagonals and can retreat as well as advance.

Capturing is achieved by hopping over an opponents piece or pieces and in order to do this the piece to be captured must have a vacant square beyond it (Figure 2). The piece hopped over or captured is taken off the board in the same move. A piece making captures may continue to move for as long as there are hostile pieces to hop over and, in doing so, the piece may change direction (Figure 3). The arrows indicate the move Black makes to capture two White men in one move.

The object of the game is to defeat your opponent by removing from the board as many of his men as possible and to immobolize any pieces he is left with. Each player moves alternately and Black always starts a game. To decide who plays Black in the first game one of the players takes a piece of each colour and conceals these in his clenched fists. He then offers his closed hands to his opponent who chooses (by pointing at or touching) one or the other. Which-

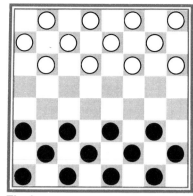

Fig. 1

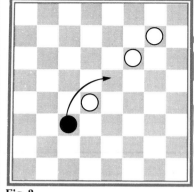

Fig. 2

ever colour is revealed to the player making the choice is the colour
he must play. Thereafter players alternate colours in subsequent
games played at the same session. Players make their moves
alternately and the rules say that if a piece is touched it must be
moved. Once a player removes his hand from a piece that has been
moved he cannot move it again until his opponent has made his
move. In other words you must make sure that you capture all the
pieces you can in one move before taking your hand off a piece.

A player who fails to take a piece that could have been taken may
be 'huffed' by his opponent. This must be done by the opponent
immediately and he can insist that the piece which should have made
the capture is removed from the board. A 'huff' is not a move and
the player who has claimed the huff then makes his own move. If
you have failed to take a piece which could be taken your opponent
does have an alternative to 'huffing' you. He can, if he chooses,
insist that you take back the move you have just made and he can
make you take the piece you have overlooked.

You may find that you have two pieces on the board which can
each make a different capture. In this case the choice is yours and
if you take a hostile piece you cannot be 'huffed' provided that the
piece you moved made all the captures available to it.

Good general advice is that when a game is under way it is
usually better to move towards the centre of the board. From here
your pieces can attack in two directions instead of being limited to
one direction from the side of the board. Always study the position
of the pieces very carefully before making a move and do not give
your opponent the chance to 'huff' you. Try to follow up the move
of a piece with other pieces to stop your opponent capturing lone
men. In other words keep your pieces up together especially
towards the end of a game. If you are ahead in captures you should
go in for equal exchanges, that is be prepared to lose a man to
capture one of his.

In competition draughts you should move within five minutes
if it is your turn otherwise your opponent may call 'Time' and then
you have only one minute to move or lose the game.

The system of recording games is quite simple and the serious
draughts player would do well to master it. Figure 4 shows the
numbering of the board. The Black squares which are the only ones
used for play are numbered from 1 to 32 starting from Black's back
row and the sequence in each row is from right to left. The Black
pieces are placed on squares 1 to 12 and White on 21 to 32. Figure 1

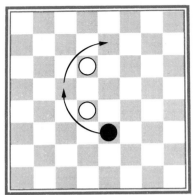

	32		31		30		29
28		27		26		25	
	24		23		22		21
20		19		18		17	
	16		15		14		13
12		11		10		9	
	8		7		6		5
4		3		2		1	

Fig. 3   **Fig. 4**

shows the pieces set up ready for a game. In Draughts diagrams Black is always shown at the bottom.

The movement of each piece is simply given as the number of the square a piece moves from followed by a dash and then the number of the square the piece finally settles on. Figure 2 shows a Black piece moving to capture a White piece. This is written as 11–18. Captures are not mentioned in the notation. As in chess, opening moves in draughts have acquired names such as the Bristol which is 11–16 or the Edinburgh 9–13. Black, who starts the play has seven moves to choose from. Thereafter his play will depend on White's moves.

Here is a game between players of equal strength which, as you might expect, ends in a draw. If you play this out on your own board you will readily see how good draughts players think ahead. Black opens with 11–15 and White replies with 23–19. Neither player can capture yet. Black's second move is 8–11 to back up the first man moved. White goes 22–17 bringing a second front row piece into play and moving to the side of the board. Black now goes 4–8 continuing to back up his front men. White continues to the side of the board with 17–13. He cannot be 'taken' here. Black ventures into enemy territory with his next move which is 15–18 and White goes 24–20.

The game proceeds as follows: 11–15, 28–24. 8–11, 26–23. 9–14, 31–26. 6–9, 13–6 (first capture). 2–9, 26–22. 1–6, 22–17. 18–22, 25–18. 15–22, 23–18. 14–23, 27–18. 9–13, 17–14. 10–17, 21–14. 6–10, 30–25. 10–17, 25–21. 22–26, 21–14. 26–30 (1st King) 19–15. 30–26, 15–8. 26–22, 32–28. 22–15, 24–19. 15–24, 28–19. 13–17, 8–4. 17–22, 4–8. 22–26, 19–15. 26–30 Drawn.

Players who tire of conventional draughts may care to try some of the variations on the game.

Losing Draughts

This game follows closely the rules and regulations of ordinary draughts except that each player aims to lose his own pieces instead of trying to capture those of his opponent. To 'huff' becomes a little different and even more important in this game and a player who fails to take a piece is made to take back his move and capture the piece or pieces he did not take. In the early moves it is safe enough to go in for equal exchanges allowing your opponent to take one of your men for each of his that you capture. Thereafter try to move

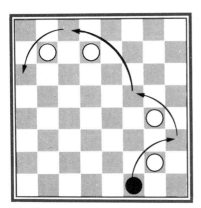

Fig. 5

your men out from your back row and leave spaces between them and the pieces in front of them. The player who first loses his pieces or cannot move those remaining on the board is the winner.

Spanish Draughts
It is usual to turn the board for this game so that each player has a Black square in the right hand corner of his back row. The pieces are set out on the Black squares as for ordinary Draughts and they move in the same way–diagonally forward. Kings, however have greater power in this game. Readers who play chess will be familiar with the Bishops' move, which is through as many squares as the player chooses provided the diagonal is clear. In Spanish draughts a King also has this 'long move' but there must be a vacant square beyond the piece the King wishes to capture so that he can hop over the piece to take it. Kings making the long move need not stay on the vacant square immediately behind the piece taken but may move on along the diagonal to any other vacant square. It is, of course, compulsory to take any pieces available in any one move. Having hopped over all pieces that are available in the one move these are then removed from the board. Once a piece reaches the opponent's back row it is crowned and remains on that square until it is the player's turn to move again. Figure 5 shows the move of a Black King to capture four White pieces in the one move. Other than this the rules for ordinary draughts apply.

German Draughts
In this game the rules of draughts apply and Kings have the same power as they have in Spanish draughts. Kings can move along a diagonal as far as the player likes provided the squares are clear and provided there is a vacant square beyond the piece the King hops over and takes. Movements of the ordinary pieces are, however a little different. They move forward on diagonals but if capturing pieces they can move backwards as well. A piece reaching the opponents back row is crowned in the ordinary way *unless* it can take more men by coming back across the board. In this case the piece continues its move and is not crowned. If there is a choice in the pieces which you can move and which will make captures, you must move the piece which can take the most hostile men in the one move.

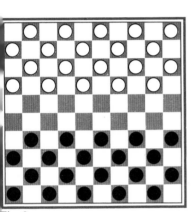

Fig. 6

Russian Draughts
This is similar to German draughts and the same rules apply except the one about pieces becoming Kings. In this game any piece reaching the opponents back row is crowned and then proceeds to complete its move by capturing any other men available to it. The players do not have to make the largest number of captures possible but are free to choose whichever piece they care to move.

Polish Draughts
This differs from the previous games described in that a board with a hundred squares is used (50 White and 50 Black). These are sometimes available in compendiums of games but the reader may find it necessary to make one. Each player has twenty pieces and the decision as to who plays Black is decided as for conventional draughts. The board is placed between the players so that each has a white square in the right hand corner nearest him. The pieces are set up as shown in Figure 6. Black has the first move.

All play is confined to the Black squares and the pieces move diagonally forward. Any piece can capture either forward or backward provided there is a vacant square beyond the piece being taken. A piece is crowned when it reaches the opponents back rank and it then becomes a Queen. As in conventional Draughts crowning is a matter of placing another piece on top of the man who then remains on the square until moved again. If a piece reaches the back rank but can still capture, it must do so and is not crowned. It is compulsory to capture the maximum pieces available. A Queen in Polish Draughts has the same powers as a King in Spanish Draughts. She is entitled to the long move, and can advance or retreat along a diagonal of squares provided they are unoccupied. She captures by hopping over an enemy piece and can either remain on the vacant square immediately beyond that piece or she can continue along other vacant squares.

Maximum capture being compulsory you would have to take an enemy Queen rather than a piece if both were available. When a Queen captures a number of pieces in one move these are left on the board until the move is completed. In this sort of move you cannot hop over the same piece twice. You may, however jump empty squares more than once in the same move. This is a refreshingly different game and one that is well worth trying.

Backgammon

Backgammon is a game in which men are moved round a board according to the throw of dice. Games with this principle have been known for at least 5,000 years, the earliest recorded example being discovered in a royal cemetery of the Sumerian civilisation in Mesopotamia.

Backgammon in most of its modern features has been played at least since the fifteenth century, and there are several backgammon boards in existence that date back to the sixteenth century. The name 'backgammon' itself dates back to 1645, though the games of 'tric-trac' (still the name used in France) and 'tables' were essentially what we know as backgammon.

However there is one very important feature of modern backgammon that was invented as recently as the 1920s, and that is the idea of *doubling*. This is a method by which the stakes can be raised during the course of the game, and it is the biggest single factor in making backgammon the action-packed game it is.

The Rules

Backgammon is a board game played between two players. Figure 1 shows the board set up in the starting position. Each player has fifteen men (variously referred to as pieces, chequers, stones) and the object of the game is to move the pieces round the board and then off the board. The player who first achieves this object is the winner.

Each player has two dice, and he makes his moves according to his dice throws.

The Board

The twenty-four elongated triangles shown in Figure 1 are referred to as 'points'. They correspond to the squares in other board games like chess or snakes and ladders. They are normally painted alternate colours to make it easier to count out the moves. There is no other significance in the different colours.

The board is divided into two halves by a central partition referred to as the 'bar'. In the configuration shown in Figure 1 the points on the right hand side of the bar make up the 'home board' and those on the left of the bar are the 'outer board'. White's home and outer boards are at the bottom of the diagram, while Black's are at the top.

The points have been numbered 1 to 12 starting from the right hand end of the board. This is to facilitate the description of the

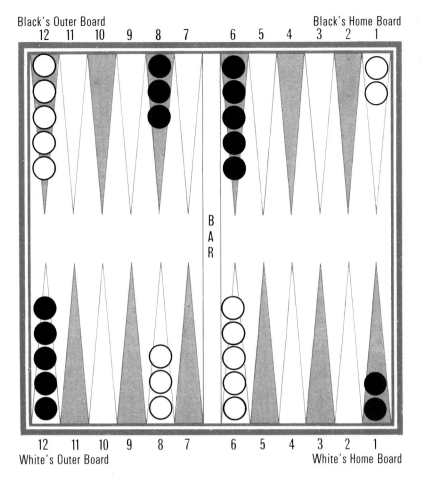

B
A
R

Fig. 1

moves; actual backgammon boards are not numbered. Points 1 to 6 are the 'home board' points, and 7 to 12 the 'outer board' points.

The Starting Position

At the beginning of a game each player sets up his men as shown in Figure 1. Notice that each player starts with five men inside his home board, on his 'six point' – i.e. on the sixth point counting from the right hand end. Each player has three men in his own outer board, on the eight point; and five men in his opponent's outer board, on the opponent's twelve point. Finally each player starts with two men in his opponent's home board, on his opponent's one point.

The player playing White sits at the bottom of the board, and Black at the top. Notice that White's home board is on his right, while Black's is on his left. The board can be set up in the mirror image position, such that White's home board is on his left. It makes no difference to the play; throughout this article we will use the set-up of Figure 1. Numbers thrown by the dice are printed in red.

The Play

Each player moves his men round the board towards his home

47

board. White moves anti-clockwise and Black clockwise. Thus the two sides are moving in opposite directions past each other. When a player has brought all his men into his home board (i.e. all his men are distributed somewhere on the points 1 to 6) he can then start to remove them from the board. The first player to remove all his men is the winner.

The players move alternately, and their moves are controlled by dice. Each player has two dice, and preferably a cup for shaking them, and when it is his turn to play he rolls the dice into the half-board on his right. Thus White rolls on the home board side of the bar, and Black on the outer board side. For a throw to be legal dice must come to rest flat on the surface of the board on the side on which they were thrown. If a die finally comes to rest on top of a man, or tilted against the side of the board, it is said to be 'cocked', and *both* dice must be thrown again.

For the first roll of the game, and the first roll only, each player throws one die. The player who rolls the higher number makes the first move, and takes as his roll the numbers shown on the two dice.

Moving the Pieces
When a player has thrown his dice, he must move his men according to the numbers showing on the dice. He considers each number separately: for example, if he rolls a 3–2 he must make a move of 3 and a move of 2, not a move of 5. If a player throws a double (i.e. 1–1, 2–2, 6–6 etc.) he must move the number four times.

There are three types of move: moving round the board, re-entering from the bar, and removing the men at the end of the game.

Moving round the board. Let us assume that the game is about to start. White throws a 5 and Black a 2, so as White has thrown the higher die he has the first move, and takes as his opening roll a 5–2. He must move one of his men five spaces, and one two spaces. He is allowed to move the same man, or he can move two different men. For example, two possible moves that White could play for his five would be to move from Black twelve point five spaces to his own eight point; or he could play a man from White eight to White three. (In future we will refer to Black's twelve point as 'B12' and so on.) For the two White could move any of his men. Figure 2 indicates the possible plays.

There are two restrictions on the movement of men round the board. The first is they cannot be moved past the one point – it is as

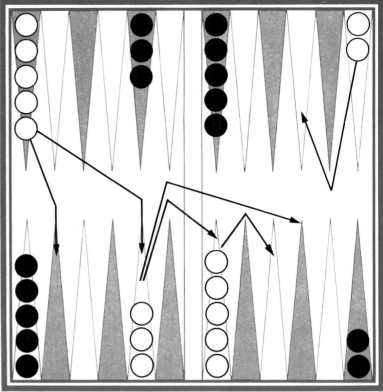

Fig. 2

if the pieces moved on a track which starts at the opponent's one point and ends at the player's own one point. For example, the men on W6 cannot be moved six spaces, as that would entail moving past W1.

The second restriction is that a man cannot be moved to a point occupied by two or more of the opponent's men. So for our example opening roll of 5−2 White could not move from B1 to B6 for the five, as B6 is already held by Black. Similarly if White played from B1 to B3 for the two, he could not then move on from B3 to B8, as B8 is also held by Black in the starting position. So in the starting position White can move from B1 with any number except a five; from B12 with any number except a one (ones being blocked by Black's men on W12); from W8 with any number; and from W6 with any number except a five or a six (fives are blocked by Black's men on W1, and a six would take the man past W1).

Re-entering moves. To introduce the second type of move, let us assume that White played his opening 5−2 by moving one man from B12 to W8, and one from B12 to W11. This leaves the situation shown in Figure 3. The isolated man at W11 is referred as a *blot*.

It is now Black's turn, and we will assume that he rolls a 6−4. One of the ways he can play the roll is to move from W1 to W5, and then onwards to W11. Remember if W11 had been occupied by two or more White men, Black would not have been able to move to that point. However, in this instance there is only one White man at W11, and in this case Black *is* allowed to move there. Furthermore, when the Black man lands on top of him the White blot is said

49

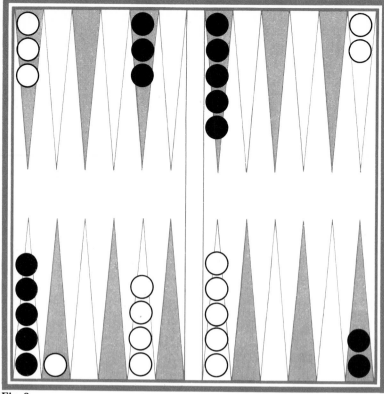

Fig. 3

to be hit. The White man is removed from the board, and has to be brought back into play at White's next turn. While the White man is in this limbo condition he is put on the bar.

When a player has a man on the bar he must bring it back into play at the first available opportunity. Until he does so he is not allowed to make any other moves. The man must be re-entered on one of the six points in the opponent's home board, as always according to the numbers shown on the dice. For example, If White has a man on the bar and he rolls a 6–2 he must re-enter the man either on B6 or on B2. As for the first type of move, he is not allowed to re-enter the man on a point held by his opponent. So if it happened that Black held B6 (as he does in the starting position) White would be forced to re-enter his man on B2. And if Black held both B6 and B2, White would not be able to re-enter at all with his 6–2, and he would lose his turn.

You will see that the more points a player manages to make in his home board the more difficult it will be for a man on the bar to re-enter. For this reason good players try to make as many home board points as possible (see below).

Bearing off. When a player has brought his men round the board and into his home, such that all fifteen of them are distributed somewhere on his own one to six point, he can start to remove them from the board. This process is called *bearing off.* As with the other types of move it is controlled by the dice, and in some respects it is the reverse process to re-entering. For example, if during the bearing off a player rolls 3–1 he is allowed to remove a man from his three point and a man from his one point, provided he has men on those points. Instead of removing a man from a given point he would also be allowed to move a man from a higher-numbered point.

An additional rule is required to cover the situation in which a player rolls a number corresponding to a vacant point. For example, a player may roll a three when he has no man on his three-point. Then if he has men on higher points he must move one of those; but if he has no men on higher numbered points he must bear off a man from the lower occupied point. This process is described more fully in the example game.

The Doubling Cube

The single feature that makes backgammon such an exciting game is the way in which the stakes can be periodically doubled during the game. The normal and most convenient way of recording the stake is with a *doubling cube*. This cube is usually rather larger than the dice, and on its six faces it has inscribed the numbers 2, 4, 8, 16, 32 and 64. At the beginning of the game the stake is one unit; as there is no 1 on the doubling cube this is signified by placing the cube half-way between the players with the 64 face uppermost.

As the game goes on, the player whose turn it is to roll may offer his opponent a 'double'. This means that the player who is doubled has the option of continuing the game at double the current stake, or of stopping the game and paying out his opponent at the current stake. If the player who is doubled accepts, the cube is turned to show twice the previous stake (e.g. to 2 for the first double of the game) and is placed on the doubled player's side of the table. The next double can only come from the player who accepted the last double.

As an example, after three rolls of a game White may decide to double. If Black accepts, the cube is turned to 2 and placed on his side of the table. The next double can only come from Black. Then if Black redoubles later in the game and White accepts, the cube is turned to 4 and placed on White's side of the table. The double to 8 can only come from White.

Scoring

In a normal game the player who first bears off all his men wins the number of points shown on the doubling cube. So if the stake was £1 a point and the cube was at 8, the winner would get £8.

A second type of win is a *gammon*. If one player removes all his men before his opponent removes any, the winning player is said to have gammoned his opponent, and he collects twice the number of points shown on the doubling cube.

A third degree of win is the *backgammon*. White would win a backgammon if Black had not removed any men and in addition still had Black men in White's home board when the last White man had been removed. In such a case Black would have to pay three times the number of points shown on the cube. In the U.K. it is quite common not to play backgammons – a player can never lose more than twice the doubling cube. Whether backgammons are played is a matter of agreement between the players.

In a normal three or four hour session between good players the margin at the end would be unlikely to be more than thirty points; between bad players it could be higher, as there tends to be more doubling cube activity in a weaker game.

An Example Game
For the opening roll, White throws a 6 and Black a 5, so as his first roll White gets a 6–5. He uses it to move a back man via Black's seven point to Black's twelve point. This will be written in shorthand:
1W. 6–5. B1–B7–B12.
It is now Black's turn, and he rolls a 3–1. He uses it to make his five point by moving a man from Black eight and one from Black six:
1B. 3–1. B8–B5, B6–B5.
The five point is the most important point to make in the early game.
2W. 6–3. B1–B7–B10.
White runs out with his other back man.
2B. 4–3. W12–B9, W12–B10 (hit).
Black hits the White blot at B9, and brings down another man into his outer board. This leaves the position shown in Figure 4.

White now has a man on the bar, and his first duty is to bring it back into play.
3W. 5–2. Bar–B2, B12–W8.
White has to re-enter on B2, and moves down from B12 with the five. Notice that if White had rolled 6–6, 6–5 or 5–5 he would not have been able to re-enter. He would then have lost his whole turn.
3B. 6–2. B10–B4, B6–B4.
Black makes another point in his home board.
4W. 5–5. B2–B7–B12, 2(W8–W3)
White is lucky in that he is able to escape with his back man to B12,

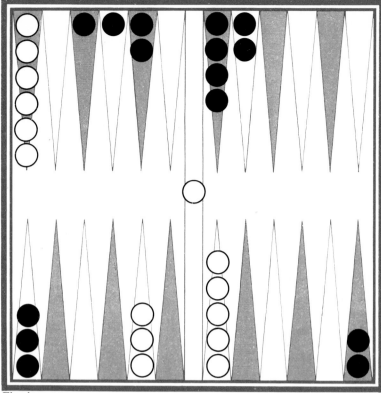

Fig. 4

and to make a point in his own home board. Remember that if you roll a double you move the number *four* times.

4B. 6−6. 2(W1−W7), W12−B7, B9−B3.

Black also gets a double, and uses it to bring his back men out to White's seven point (or *bar point*) and to move two other men towards home.

5W. 5−1. B12−W8, W6−W5.

White brings one man down and starts his five point. Now that both sides have rescued their back men they will try to avoid leaving blots where their opponent could hit them. Since the blot on W5 is behind Black's rear-most men it is safe.

5B. 4−4. 2(W7−W11−B10)

Black manages to escape from White's bar point.

6W. 6−5. B12−W7, B12−W8.

6B. 5−4. W12−B8, W12−B9.

7W. 3−3. 2(W8−W5), 2(B12−W10).

This leaves the position shown in Figure 5. In the last three moves both players are simply moving round the board and getting their men in as fast as possible. To accelerate this rather boring phase of the game we will give both sides double sixes:

7B. 6−6. 2(B10−B4), B9−B3, B8−B2.

8W. 6−6. 2(W10−W4), B12−W7, W8−W2.

8B. 5−5. 2(B8−B3), B7−B2, B5−off.

Black brings his last three men into his home board. Having done that, he still has one five to play, and he bears off a man from his five point.

9W. 6−2. W7−W1, W8−W6.

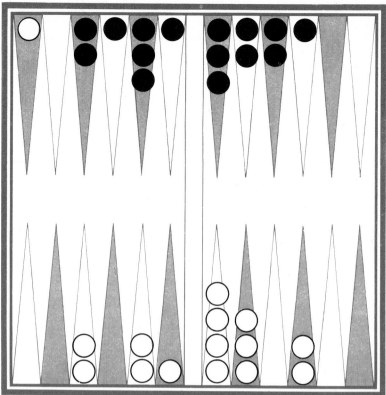

Fig. 5

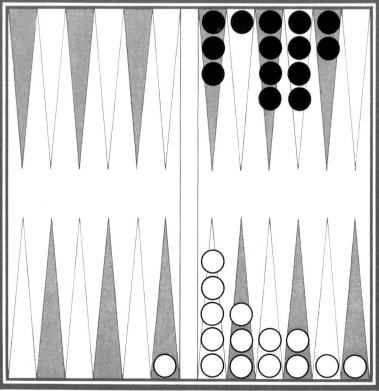

Fig. 6

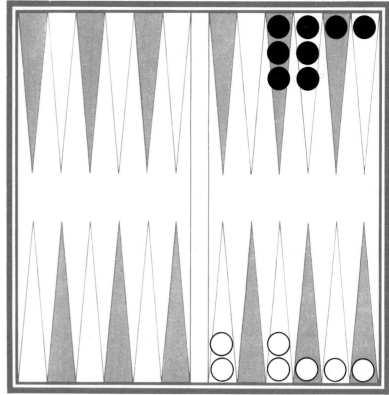

Fig. 7

This leaves the position shown in Figure 6.

Up to this stage neither side has had much of an advantage. But Black's 5−5 makes him a distinct favourite; it is now his turn to roll, but before he does so he *doubles*. White has the option of either conceding one point and getting on with the next game, or of playing on with the stake now at two points. White choses to accept, whereupon he takes the doubling cube over to his side of the table and turns it to 2.

9B. 5−1. B5−off, B6−B5.

Black takes a man off from the five point; since he has no man on the one point he must move a man from a higher point for the one. He chooses to move from the six point.

10W. 2−1. W7−W5, W1−off.

A miserable roll for White. He brings in his remaining man to his five point and takes a man off the one point.

10B. 5−3. B5−off, B3−off.

11W 6−3. W6−off, W3−off.

11B. 5−2. B6−B1, B2−off.

Black has no man on the five, so as he has a man on a higher point (i.e. the six point) he must move from there.

12W. 6−5. W6−off, W5−off.

12B. 6−4. B6−off, B4−off.

13W. 5−5. 3(W5−off), W6−W1.

White takes off his three men on the five point, and then has to move from the six point with the five. This leaves the position shown in Figure 7.

13B. 5−4. 2(B4−off).

Now a new rule comes into operation. Black has no man on his five point, but since he also has no man on a higher point he must bear off a man from the next lower occupied point – in this position, his four point.

14W. 5 – 5. 2(W6 – W1), 2(W4 – off).

For his first pair of 5s White has to move to his one point; but for the second pair, as he now has no more men on his six point he is allowed to take two men off his four point.

14B. 5 – 4. B4 – off, B3 – off.

15W. 6 – 2. W3 – off, W2 – off.

15B. 2 – 1. B2 – off, B1 – off.

This leaves the following position: White, three men on W1. Black, two men on B3. It is White's turn to roll, but as he is now favourite, before he rolls he doubles. Black accepts, so the doubling cube goes back to Black's side of the table at 4.

16W. 2 – 1. 2(W1 – off).

White would have won the game outright if he had rolled a double at throw 16. He is still slightly favoured, as Black will not get off if he rolls a one or a two (apart from double 2).

16B. 6 – 1. B3 – off, B3 – B2.

Black fails to get both men off. Since White is bound to get his man off now, White wins and receives four points (the number showing on the doubling cube).

This was rather a tedious game as there was only one hit in the whole game (Black's move 2), and both sides managed to get their back men out easily.

More exciting games occur when there is more blot hitting and when one side or the other manages to block in their opponent's back men.

The Elements of Good Play

The object of the game is for a player to remove all his pieces before his opponent. There are two broad ways in which the player can approach this objective: he can do so directly, by simply running his men round the board at every opportunity while taking little notice of what his opponent is doing; or he can take a more indirect line, and play to slow down his opponent by forming barriers and hitting blots wherever possible. If a player follows either of these techniques exclusively, he will probably lose. In most games a good player will use a combination of these tactics, adapting his game to suit the situation.

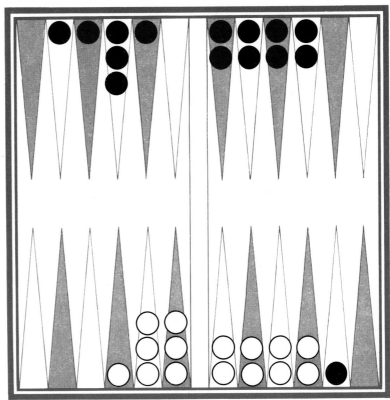

Fig. 8

Blocks and primes. The most powerful blockade against an opponent is six points in a row. Look at Figure 8. The Black man on W2 cannot move as all the points between one and six spaces away from him are held by White. (Remember, if Black throws say a 6–4, he cannot play a ten but must move a separate six and four.) White's succession of points running from W8 down to W3 is called a *prime*.

The lesson to be learnt from this is that it is a good thing to build up groups of consecutive points. In the starting position each player already holds two good points for blocking (his eight and six points), and much early play revolves round building up a block starting with this framework.

Home board points. Look at Figure 9. It is Black's turn and he has a man on the bar. He needs to get specifically a 1 to re-enter his man, odds of about five to two against. But change the position by moving the two men on W2 back to W7 and those on W3 to W8, and now Black only needs a 1, 2 or 3 to re-enter, odds of three to one on. The message here is that the more home board points a player has, the more serious it is for his opponent to be hit. So good players build up their home board whenever they can.

Blots. Clearly when the opponent has a strong home board a player will try to avoid leaving blots where they can be hit. But it is a mistake to play too cautiously, particularly in the early part of the game, and it is often good play in the first few moves to leave blots in order to gain greater flexibility. In a high quality game most of the risks are taken early on.

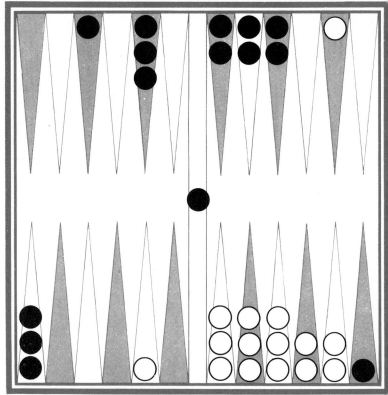

Fig. 9

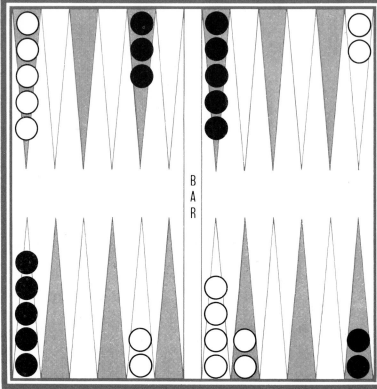

Fig. 10

The Opening Moves

This general preamble brings us on to the best way of playing the early rolls. This is quite an instructive topic, as many of the ideas are useful for the later parts of the game.

The opening rolls fall into three principal categories: (i) point-making rolls, which are ones that enable the player to make a useful point immediately; (ii) extrication rolls, which are used to start the back men on the road to freedom; (iii) building rolls, which are used to set up the men to make a useful point at the player's second turn. We will consider them all from White's point of view.

Point-making rolls. 3–1, 6–1, 4–2, 5–3.
With all these rolls it is best to make a point down in the vital area of the board between W8 and W3.
3–1. W8–W5, W6–W5. Figure 10 shows the play of this most desirable opening roll. The five point is the most important point, as it adds to the block already started by W8 and W6, and on top of this is a home board point.
6–1. B12–W7, W8–W7. This roll enables White to make his seven point, or *bar point*. The bar point is the best purely blocking point, as it fills in the gap between the points already held; and as it is six spaces away from Black's back men it blocks 6–6 and 6–5, the best escaping rolls.
4–2. W8–W4, W6–W4. Like the five-point, the four point pulls weight in two ways, as a blocker and as a homeboard point.
5–3. W8–W3, W6–W3. Not such a good point, as it is too far forward to have much blocking effect. However it improves in strength if White subsequently makes his five or four point.

Running rolls. 6–5, 6–4, 6–3.
All are played by running out a back man from B1. With a 6–5 the man gets to safety at B12, with the other two White has to leave a blot either at B11 or B10.

Building rolls. 6–2, 5–1, 4–1, 2–1; 5–4, 5–2, 4–3, 3–2.
None of these rolls does anything appetising immediately; they are used to prepare the ground for making a point at the next turn.
6–2, 5–1, 4–1, 2–1. All these rolls are used to put a blot onto the five point, the idea being that if it is not hit by Black at his first turn White may be able to cover it at his second turn.
6–2: B12–W11–W5.

5−1 : B12−W8, W6−W5.
4−1 : B12−W9, W6−W5.
2−1 : B12−W11, W6−W5.
5−4, 5−2, 4−3, 3−2. All these rolls are played by moving two men from B12 down into White's outer board. The idea is that if the blot or blots so exposed survive, White will be well placed to make a good point at his next turn.

The play of doubles. The rules do not allow the first player to get doubles. If the second player gets a double as his first roll, the best way to play them is as follows (again from White's point of view).
6−6. 2(B1−B7), 2(B12−W7). White makes both bar points. A good roll.
5−5. 2(B12−W8−W3). White makes his three point from White's twelve point. But if Black had split his back men at his first turn, then it is usually better to play 2(W8−W3), 2(W6−W1) if by so doing White can put a Black man onto the bar.
4−4. 2(B1−B5), 2(B12−W9). White makes Black's five point, a powerful point for defensive operations; and brings down two men into his own blockade.
3−3. 2(W8−W5), 2(W6−W3). White makes two good home board points.
2−2. 2(B12−W11), 2(W6−W4). White brings down two builders, makes a home board point.
1−1. 2(W8−W7), 2(W6−W5). An extremely fine roll, as it enables White to make his bar and five points immediately.

Another consideration in the first few rolls is that it may be possible to hit an opponent's blot. It is usually correct to do so anywhere outside the player's own home board.

Otherwise the players concentrate on the twin themes of extricating their own back men while attempting to trap the opponent's back men.

Other Forms of the Game
Chouette. Though normally backgammon is played between two people, it is possible for more people to play in one game. In such a case one player (the 'man in the box') plays by himself against the others. One of the other players is called the 'captain'. If the captain's side wins a game, the captain becomes the man in the box, the next person in the queue becomes the captain, and the previous man in the box goes to the bottom of the queue. If the man in the

box wins, he stays in the box and the captaincy is taken over by the next in line. The players can debate amongst themselves the best way to play a particular roll, or whether or not to double, but the captain has the deciding vote. While the players cannot double the box individually, they may accept or refuse the box's doubles individually.

Tournaments. Backgammon tournaments are becoming increasingly popular. The usual form is to play a knock-out. The winner of each match in the various rounds of the knock-out is the first player to reach a given number of points. The winners of each match are paired against each other in the successive rounds, until finally there is only one unbeaten player.

Go

Most Go players believe that theirs is the most interesting and profound of all board games. Go has been played for thousands of years in the Far East, but it is only in the last decade or two that it has achieved international status, with national Go organisations in most Western countries. The basic rules are simple and elegant, yet the number of possible developments is so astronomically large that the game can never become stereotyped or predictable.

The Equipment

A standard size Go board is ruled with 19 × 19 horizontal and vertical lines (Figure 1). Play takes place on the 361 points of intersection of these lines, and not on the squares. A theoretically limitless supply of black and white men known as 'stones' are used for

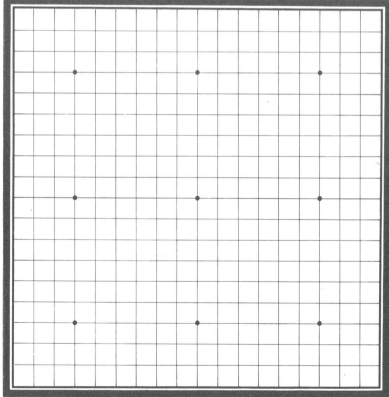

Fig. 1

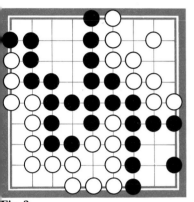

Fig. 2

play. Traditional Japanese stones are bi-convex in shape, and beautifully made from slate and shell. A full set comprises 181 black and 180 white stones. Western players are usually less particular about their equipment, and often improvise sets from counters, buttons, drawing pins, etc., and boards made of hardboard or card.

The Moves
Play starts with the board empty. Players move alternately, Black playing first. A move consists of placing a stone on any unoccupied intersection of the board, subject to two restrictions described below. Once played stones are not moved unless they are captured by the opponent's in which case they are removed from the board. Thus the board gradually fills up with stones during a game.

The Object
The primary object of the game is to surround vacant space on the board, with a secondary object of capturing the opponent's stones. When the end of the game is reached each player scores one point for each unoccupied intersection on the board that he surrounds with his stones (usually referred to as his 'territory') plus one point for each enemy stone captured. The player with the higher total score wins. The margin of points is not regarded as important—a win by a single point carries the same credit as a win by 100.

Figure 2 shows the end of a game played on a 9×9 board. (Smaller boards such as this are often used by beginners or those who want just a quick game.) Black has surrounded nine vacant points near the upper edge, five near the lower right corner, and an odd one in the middle making 15 in all. White has eight in the upper right corner, six in the lower left corner, and one near the lower edge, also totalling 15. However, the game was not tied as Black captured one white stone during the game while White made no capture, so Black won by 16 points to 15.

It is important to note that it is the *vacant* points which count as territory, not the ones actually occupied by the stones, and that points along the edge and in the corner all count as territory.

Captures
Captures are made by closely surrounding enemy stones. A single stone in the middle of the board is said to have four 'liberties', i.e. the four horizontally and vertically adjacent points marked with

crosses in Figure 3a. If at any time the opponent can occupy all four of these points with his stones the original stone is captured. Figure 3b shows the black stone with only one liberty left, and 3c shows the position after White occupies the last liberty and removes the stone. Stones removed like this are retained as 'prisoners' by the player who makes the capture, to add to his score at the end of the game.

Figure 4a shows how a stone on the edge of the board has only three liberties, and one in the corner has only two. Figure 4b shows the positions after White has occupied the liberties of these stones and captured them.

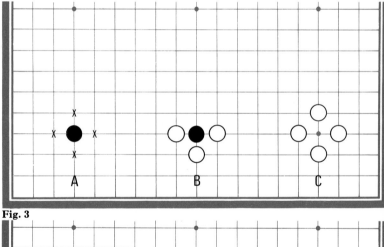

Fig. 3

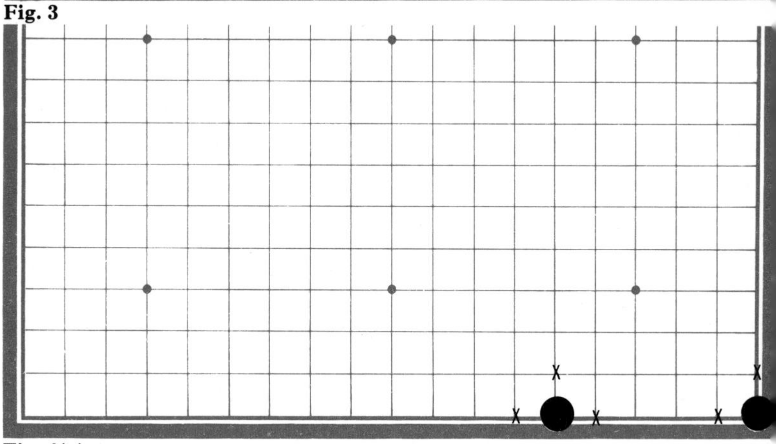

Fig. 4(a)

Armies

If a player plays a stone on a liberty of one of his own stones already on the board, the two form a connected unit called an army (see Figure 5a). Armies can be extended in size without limit by connection via liberties. Further examples of armies are given in Figures 5b, c and d. It is important to realise that diagonally adjacent stones are not connected. The two white armies in Figure 6 would require another stone at 'x' or 'y' to connect them into a single unit.

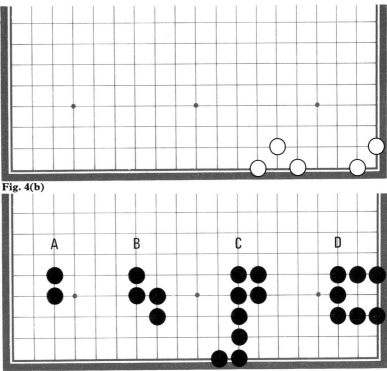

Fig. 4(b)

Fig. 5

The Capture of Armies

Armies have more liberties than single stones, but the principle involved in capturing them is similar. When the last remaining liberty is occupied by an enemy stone the whole army is removed at once—it cannot be captured piecemeal. Figure 7 shows the armies in Figure 5 with all their liberties bar one (marked with 'x') occupied by enemy stones, i.e. subject to capture on the next move. (Go players often use the Japanese term 'atari' to describe this situation – chess players will recognise the analogy with 'en prise'.) If the opponent is able to occupy this last liberty each army is captured and immediately removed from the board, leading to the positions shown in Figure 8. Note that armies such as 5*d* with an internal space have to be surrounded internally as well as externally before they are captured.

It is worth mentioning one of the basic tactical principles of Go at this stage. Clearly the more liberties an army has the harder it is to capture. It is therefore usually good play to separate your opponent's stones into small units as much as possible, while keeping your own in positions where they may be easily linked together if necessary.

The Suicide Rule
As mentioned above, there are two prohibitive rules in Go. The first of these, the 'Suicide Rule', forbids a player to play so as to leave any of his own stones or armies with no liberty, i.e. in the sort of position where they would be captured if the opponent had brought it about. To put it another way, he must not capture his own stones.

Points 'a', 'b', and 'c' in Figure 9 are all examples of illegal moves for White. A play at 'a' would leave that stone with no liberty; a play at 'b' would leave a three-stone army with no liberty; and a play at 'c' would unite the white stones into a five-stone army with no liberty. However, point 'd' represents a different case, as by

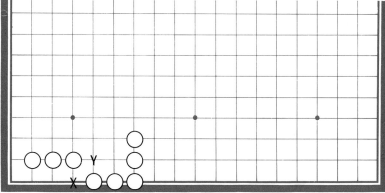

Fig. 6

66

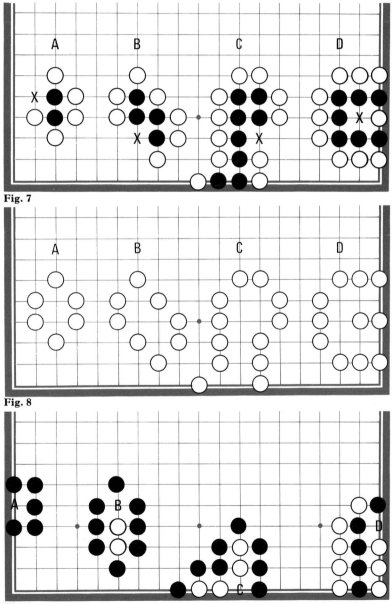

Fig. 7

Fig. 8

Fig. 9

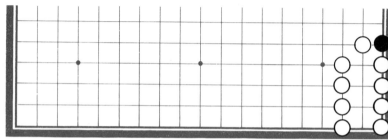

Fig. 10

playing there White captures some black stones and creates some new liberties for his army. In cases like this the move is permitted. Figure 10 shows the position resulting from this move and the capture of four black stones.

The Ko Rule

The second prohibitive rule is designed to prevent repetition of the same position. Its name derives from the Japanese word 'Ko', which signifies 'eternity'. Figure 11a shows when it applies. White may capture at 'x' if he wishes, leading to the position in Figure 11b. The move is not suicide, as he has created a new liberty for his stone at 'y'. If Black were now to recapture at 'y', this move would lead straight back to the position in Figure 11a. However, the Ko rule forbids him to make this recapture immediately; he must make at least one move elsewhere on the board first. This will give White the chance to end the Ko situation if he wishes by playing at 'y' himself on his next move, leading to Figure 11c. If White chooses to play elsewhere on the board, Black will be at liberty to recapture at 'y' whenever he wishes. Locally this will repeat the position, but over the board as a whole the position will have been altered by the addition of at least one stone of each colour.

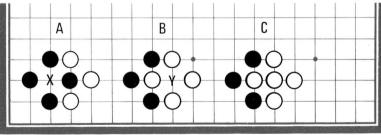

Fig. 11

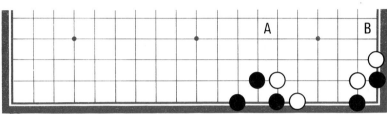

Fig. 12

Figures 12*a* and *b* show how Ko positions can occur on the edge of the board or in the corner.

The rule states further that if, despite the prohibition, the same position should occur twice in a game, the game is drawn. This can only occur in certain specialised positions which will occur very rarely.

The End of the Game
The theoretical formula for ending the game is that either player may at any time pass his turn to play, and when both players pass in succession the game ends. If one player wishes to continue making moves while the other passes, the passing player should surrender one stone from his supply to his opponent as a prisoner for each move passed.

In practice, however, experienced players nearly always end their games by mutual agreement, when both can see that further moves cannot benefit either of them. This point is reached when all the available territory has been securely surrounded either by black or by white stones, and when there is no doubt in either player's mind whether or not a particular stone or army can be captured.

If one player does pass, while his opponent continues to move, one of the players is making a mistake. If the player who is still making moves is not increasing his score thereby he is wasting his time; if he *is* increasing his score then his opponent should not be passing but making suitable counter-moves.

End-of-game Customs
There are certain customs associated with the end of the game which, while not embodied in the rules, are usually observed by Go players.

When the game is nearing its end there are usually a number of 'neutral points'—a sort of no man's land between opposing armies which cannot be surrounded by either player and where it is of no significance who plays. When there are no better moves available than these neutral points they are usually filled in very rapidly by the players without taking strict turns. Figure 13 shows the game in Figure 2 at the stage just before the filling in of neutral points– the points marked 'x' were filled in in the manner described.

After filling in neutral points it is customary for each player to allow his opponent to remove from the board as captives any stones which, although still on the board, he acknowledges to be in a hopeless position where they could not escape ultimate capture if the game were to continue further. These now count as prisoners along with other stones captured during play. Such stones are often referred to as 'virtually dead' while they remain on the board.

Territories are then rearranged into convenient rectangles for ease of counting. Prisoners are usually used to fill up the opponent's territory, as the margin of points will be the same whether they are added to their captor's territory or subtracted from the opponent's. Figure 14 shows the game in Figure 2 rearranged in this way, with the white captive used to fill up a point of White's territory.

An Actual Game

The game shown in Figure 15 was played by two players of intermediate strength. It has been chosen because the strategy is very simple and it is free from any gross blunders, although the moves chosen were not always the best. To understand it it is best to play the moves through in order on a board.

Moves 1–5. These moves take advantage of the fact that territory is easiest to acquire in the corners and along the edge.

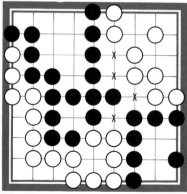
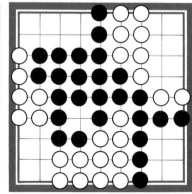

Fig. 13   Fig. 14

White 6. This tries to reduce the size of Black's potential territory sketched out with 1, 3, and 5.

7 and 8. Black counterattacks and White strengthens his own framework along the lower edge.

9–15. Now Black makes a series of threats to enter the potential white territory. White consolidates, but after his 15 White 6 is cut off from the main group. Both players know that this stone cannot now avoid ultimate capture, so both leave it alone. White does not wish to waste more stones in a hopeless rescue attempt, and there is no hurry for Black to effect the capture.

16 and 17. White 6 still has an effect on the game. White 16 threatened a further play at the point Black occupied with his move 17, which would have left the black stones 9, 11, 13, and 15 with no means of escaping capture, so Black had to protect himself.

18–21. White expands his territory and reduces Black's, while Black prevents any further incursion and prepares a counter-offensive.

22–24. White carries out a similar operation on the other side of the board.

25. A good move – the intention behind his 21. White would like to cut this stone off from Black 21 by playing at the point occupied by 27, but Figure 16 shows the disaster that would ensue for White. So he has to play defensively at 26 and 28, after which Black will be immediately captured if he plays at 'x'.

Figure 16: this Black 27 cuts off five white stones and places them in 'atari'. They are then virtually dead – even if the sequence continues up to Black 31 White cannot escape as Black has the altern-

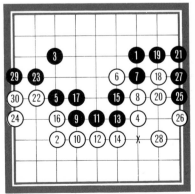

Fig. 15

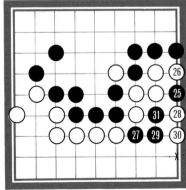

Fig. 16

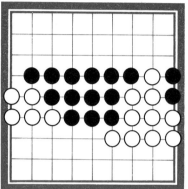

Fig. 17

atives of capturing at '25' or at 'x' if White connects at '25' himself.

Moves 29–30 (Figure 15). These moves fill the last remaining gaps in the defensive chains around the players' territories. There were no neutral points in this game. White now allowed Black to remove the virtually dead stone White 6 as a captive. The territories were rearranged as in Figure 17, the white captive being used to occupy a point of white territory. Black won by five points.

Many games of Go are more complex than this one, with the territories more fragmented, and perhaps more stones being captured, but one does sometimes find this simple style of play in master games.

Secure Territory

Beginners often find it hard to know when a certain area can be regarded as secure territory, or whether additional stones are needed to secure it. A useful definition of secure territory is as follows: a player can regard any area as securely surrounded if he is sure of being able to capture any enemy stone that should be played within it. Figure 18a shows a secure Black area of six points–no further black stones are needed here. If White tries to invade as in Figure 18b, Black can capture White's stones. After Black 4 White cannot play at either 'x' or 'y' because of the suicide rule, and as Black could take off the white stones at any time with a play at 'x' they are virtually dead.

Figure 19a shows territory that is not yet quite secure–Black can press back White's frontiers somewhat as shown in Figure 19b,

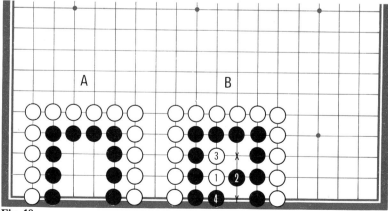

Fig. 18

reducing the territory by a couple of points. (I leave the reader to examine why White 6 is needed.)

Figure 20*a* shows a worse form of insecurity. At first sight there appear to be no gaps in White's border, but when Black plays at 1 in Figure 20*b* three white stones are in 'atari' and have no means to avoid capture. (If White plays on the point occupied by Black 5 he loses four stones instead of three.) So the best White can do now is to let these stones go, and save what territory he can with his 2 and 4. Black 5 captures the three stones. Of course White needed a play at 'x' in Figure 20*a* to secure all the territory.

Secure territory is an area where neither player should play stones.

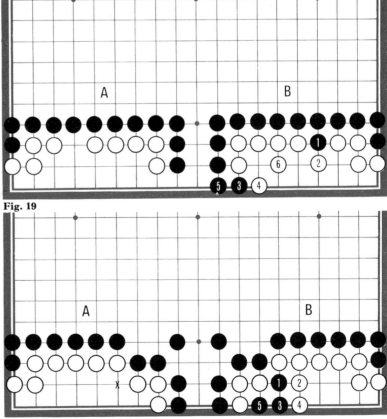

Fig. 19

Fig. 20

If a player puts stones within his own secure territory, he reduces his score by one point for each stone he plays there (remember, it is only the *vacant* points that count). If he puts them within his opponent's secure territory, then by the above definition they become virtually dead as soon as played. Even if he forces the opponent to make defensive moves within his territory, thereby filling in his own points, he is still supplying him with an extra prisoner for each defensive move he forces him to make, leaving the final score unchanged. (See Figure 18 for an example of this process.)

A Common Misconception

Beginners sometimes imagine that by refusing to surrender virtually dead stones at the end of the game, and insisting on the opponent's occupying all their liberties before removing them, he can be forced to fill in extra points within his own territory. All the opponent would need to do in such a case would be to wait until the neutral points were all filled and then proceed with filling in the liberties of the virtually dead stones. What is the first player to do meanwhile? If he passes, he will have to surrender a prisoner to his opponent each move: if he plays, he must either play within his own territory or his opponent's, in each case losing one point each play. The result must always be to leave the final score unchanged.

If you examine the final positions shown in Figures 2 and 15 you can confirm that neither player can play again anywhere without incurring a loss of one point. This stage is always the end of the game.

Basic Capturing Techniques

Certain methods of capturing stones are so common that every Go player needs to be aware of them.

When a single stone is in 'atari' in the middle of the board (see Figure 21a), it can at least temporarily avoid capture by a play on its own last liberty (i.e. at 'x'). But when this situation occurs on the second line, facing the edge (Figure 21b), adding further stones does no good at all, as the sequence in Figure 21c shows. The stone was virtually dead to start with, and White has only increased his loss in trying to save it.

Figure 22a shows another common position. After Black plays at 'x' there is no way to save the white stone, as Figure 22b illustrates.

Figure 23a shows an interesting capture called the 'ladder attack'. If Black is foolish enough to try to save his single stone with a play

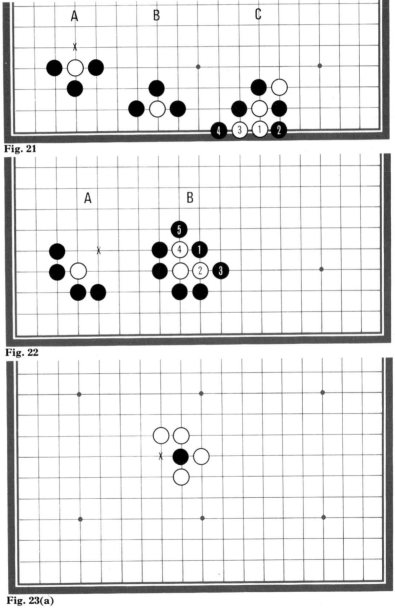

Fig. 21

Fig. 22

Fig. 23(a)

75

at 'x', and then persists in this policy, Figure 23*b* shows how with each move White can keep the growing black army in 'atari', until the sequence reaches the board's edge. White 24 then captures the 13-stone army, and such a loss in an actual game would usually call for Black's immediate resignation.

In Figure 23*c* there is a black stone 'x' in the path of the ladder attack. In this case Black can rescue his attacked stone, and it is White that would be wrong to persist with the attack – Figure 23*d* shows what will happen. After Black 15 he can no longer place Black in 'atari', and his own stones are now very vulnerable to capture with moves such as 'y' and 'z' which place two stones in 'atari' at once.

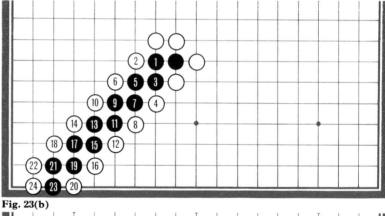

Fig. 23(b)

Fig. 23(c)

A white stone in the path of the ladder can cause it to end before the edge of the board (see Figure 23e). As misjudged ladder attacks cause such immense losses, understanding them is an important part of a Go player's tactical skill.

Invulnerable Armies

Figure 18b shows a particular case of a general rule about armies that are permanently safe from capture. We have seen from Figure 5d that an army with an internal space has to be surrounded internally as well as externally to be captured. Because of the suicide rule, the play which actually captures the army must be on one of the internal liberties. If White had tried to occupy all the internal

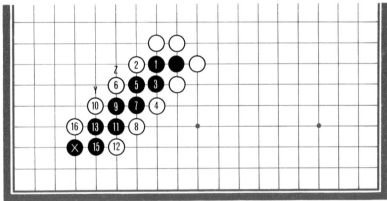

Fig. 23(d)

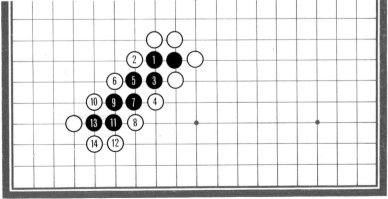

Fig. 23(e)

liberties first, as shown in Figure 24, he would have contravened the suicide rule with White 2. Such moves are only permitted when they have the effect of capturing the army, i.e. when all the external liberties are already filled.

If this army had a second, separate internal space, as shown in Figure 25a, then White has no way to effect the capture. He can fill up all the external liberties and all except one liberty within each space as shown in Figure 25b, but either of the moves 'x' and 'y' would now be suicide and illegal. He cannot play 'x' until he has played 'y' and he cannot play 'y' until he has played 'x'! Any army that has two *separate* spaces like this is permanently safe from capture. This tactical principle is of fundamental importance.

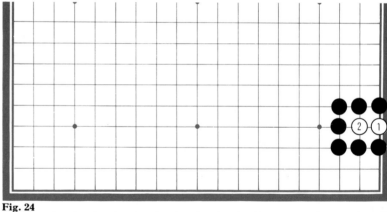

Fig. 24

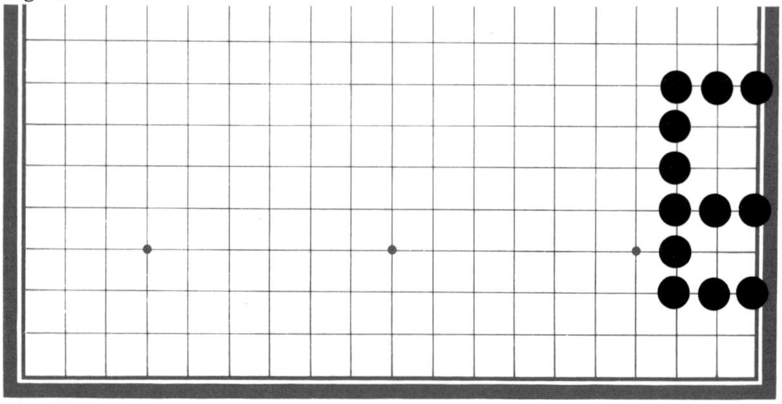

Fig. 25(a)

Figure 26 shows further examples of invulnerable black armies. The two separate spaces are often referred to as the army's 'eyes'. Eyes can be of any size, and they may or may not contain some virtually dead enemy stones.

False Eyes

Figure 27a shows two examples of white armies with so-called 'false eyes'. At first they appear to be invulnerable, but some of the stones are not properly connected (remember that there are no connections along diagonals), and part of each group can be captured separately. Plays at 'x' and 'y' lead to the positions in Figure 27b where each army has clearly only one eye.

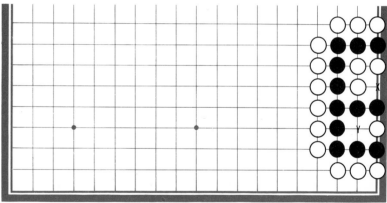

Fig. 25(b)

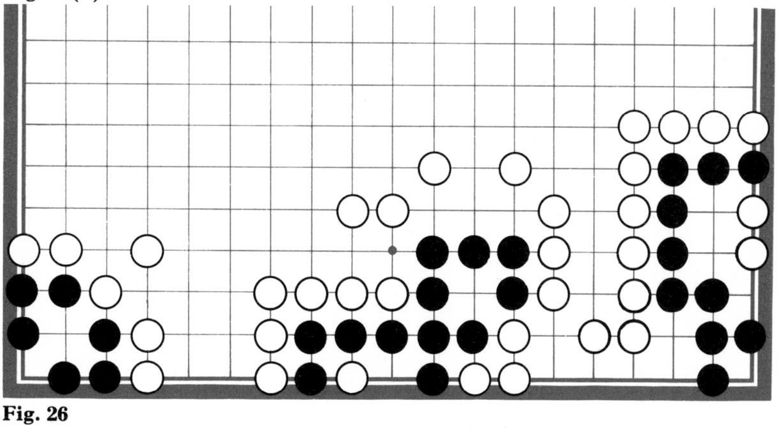

Fig. 26

When to Make Eyes

Any army with a large internal space can be fairly certain of being able to divide it in two in the event of an attack, and it is bad play to waste stones making two eyes before it becomes really necessary. All the armies in Figures 2 and 15 are invulnerable – indeed, it is one of the features of the end of the game that every army on the board must be invulnerable or virtually dead.

However, when the internal space is a small one, the ability to make two eyes becomes critical. Figure 28*a* shows an army with only three internal points, and Black must at once play 'x' to save his army. If he fails to do so White will play there himself as in

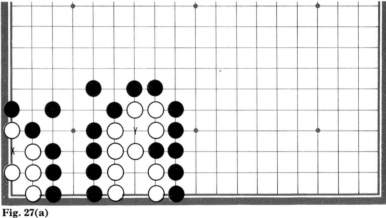

Fig. 27(a)

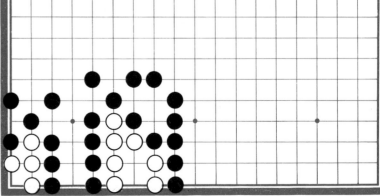

Fig. 27(b)

Figure 28*b*. Black may capture this one stone as in Figure 28*c*, but now White could play back at 'x' and capture the whole army. If the army had some external liberties White could not capture it at once, but it would still be virtually dead. Figure 29*a* shows another example. If Black plays at 'x' he has two eyes; if White plays there as in Figure 29*b* Black's attempt to divide his territory in two is doomed to failure.

Figure 30 shows a black army that does not require another stone for safety. It has only one eye at present, but if White plays at 'x' to try to prevent the formation of two eyes Black just plays at 'y', or vice versa.

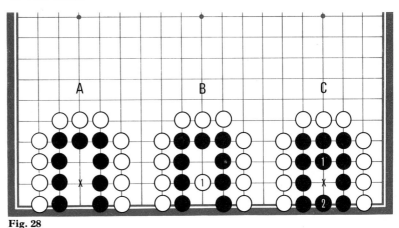

Fig. 28

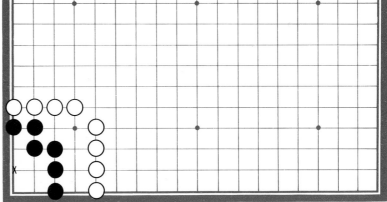

Fig. 29(a)

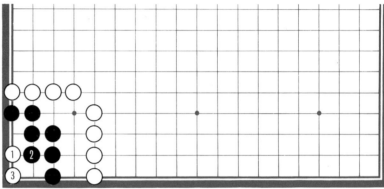

Fig. 29(b)

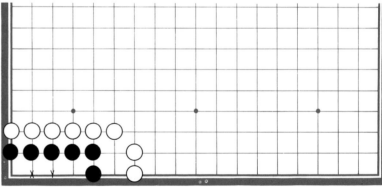

Fig. 30

Over-large Territories

Sometimes a territory is so large, or has so many weaknesses in its boundary, that there is room for the opponent to play inside it and make an invulnerable army. Figure 31*a* shows how White could invade a rather improbable Black territory. The sequence up to 5 is a standard corner opening, and the white stones will have no trouble in making two eyes in the corner should Black continue his attack. However, White can easily capture any black stones played in his territory in Figure 31*b*—there is not enough space for Black to make two eyes if White makes appropriate counter-moves.

Life and Death Struggles

Sometimes two armies are in such a position that neither can make two eyes without capturing the other. Such a position is described

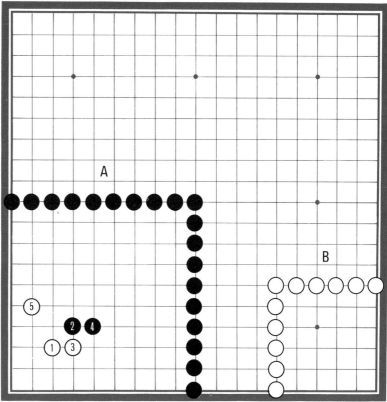

Fig. 31

by the Japanese word 'semeai'. Figure 32*a* shows a black and a white army of five stones each neither of which can break through the encircling enemy stones and neither of which can make even one eye without capturing the enemy army. In cases like this it is generally the army with the more liberties that wins the struggle. Here Black has four liberties and White only three, so even if White plays first Black wins the fight. With Black 6 in Figure 32*b* he captures the five white stones, thereby making his own safe.

In an actual game the players would not play out these moves as both would know that this fight must inevitably be won by Black, and therefore the white stones are already virtually dead.

When the fighting armies have some common liberties, there can be a rather surprising result. Figure 33*a* shows a position similar to

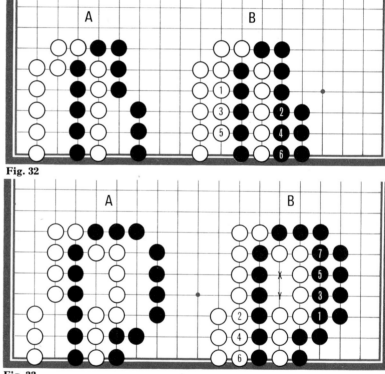

Fig. 32

Fig. 33

Figure 32a, and as White's stones have six liberties to the black stones' five, you might expect White to win the fight even when Black moves first. However, after Black 7 in Figure 33b White dare not play on one of the common liberties 'x' and 'y' as he would be immediately captured by his opponent's play on the other. When it is Black's turn, he dare not play on either of these points for the same reason. The position has reached a local stalemate (often known by the Japanese term 'seki') and the players will leave the stones as they are until the end of the game. The points 'x' and 'y' will be filled in then as neutral points, but neither army is regarded as captured.

In a case like this the moves might well be played out in an actual game. If Black fails to play 1, White will still play at 2 and then he will be one liberty ahead, and in time to capture the black army.

There are other types of seki, and I leave the reader to investigate for himself the relative numbers of external and common liberties required to produce a seki. It is also interesting to examine the effect on life-and-death struggles if one or both armies has a single eye.

One rule about the seki needs to be mentioned. If a seki is left on the board at the end of a game (as it usually would be) territory surrounded by the two armies is not counted towards the scores.

Ko-fights

In the Ko position already shown in Figures 11 and 12, usually only one stone is at stake. As it takes two plays to capture and keep one stone in such a position, it is not very profitable as a manoeuvre, and is usually left right until the end of the game.

However, sometimes more is at stake than one stone. Figure 34a shows a position where the fate of a whole army depends on the outcome of a Ko position. White would like to play at 'x', making one of the black army's eyes into a false one, so that the army would be virtually dead.

It is Black to play, however, and he will of course capture at 'x' leading to Figure 34b. If he could play at 'y' on his next move his army would have two good eyes and be invulnerable. White can only prevent this by recapturing at 'y', but the Ko rule prevents his doing this at once. What is White to do?

White must make some threat, elsewhere on the board, that is so compelling that Black must answer it at once, in preference to

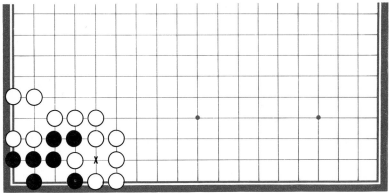

Fig. 34(a)

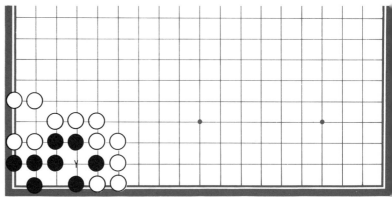

Fig. 34(b)

playing at 'y'. After Black has answered it, White will be allowed to recapture at 'y', leading back to Figure 34*a*. If Black does not want to give up the struggle, it will then be his turn to seek a 'Ko-threat'.

Let us see how this works in an actual game. Figure 35*a* shows a game nearing its end, but with the Ko position of Figure 34*a* still unresolved in the lower left corner. If Black can make two eyes for his army there he will have at least ten points (two in that corner, seven in the lower right area plus one prisoner), while White has only nine (four in the top left corner, four in the middle left area plus one prisoner already taken), and Black will win.

Black 1 captures at 'x' (see Figure 35*b*) and White plays at 2 as a Ko-threat. This move threatens to cut off and capture nine black

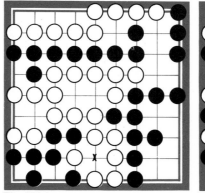

Fig. 35(a)

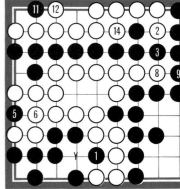

Fig. 35(b)

stones, giving White an easy victory. Therefore Black must answer at 3 in preference to playing 'y'. White 4 recaptured Black 1 in the Ko at 'y', and now Black needed a strong threat himself to stop White killing his army on the next move. Black 5 sufficed, as it threatened to capture two white stones, thereby making the necessary second eye and taking some white territory away. So White had to answer at 6, and with his 7 Black could now capture at '1' once again. White's next Ko threat 8 threatened thirteen black stones, so Black 9 was essential, and White could recapture at 'y' once again with his 10. Black 11 threatened to stop White from making two eyes for his corner army (cf. Figure 30) so White played 12 to make them. Black 13 recaptured at '1' in the Ko yet again, but then White had no further Ko-threat available. All he could do was to fill in a neutral point such as 14. So Black filled in the Ko at 'y' with his 15, made his second eye, and won the game by one point. If White had had one more threat available, he would have won the Ko-fight and the game, as Black had no more threats himself.

Ko-fights can be very complex if they occur in the middle game, when many threats are available. Plays such as Black 5 and 11 are quite pointless as ordinary moves as they gain nothing, but as stalling moves to enable the player to recapture in the Ko without infringing the Ko rule they are very valuable.

Efficiency
Since both players play the same number of stones, but one ends with more territory than the other, he must have used his stones more efficiently than his opponent, i.e. he has a better ratio of stones

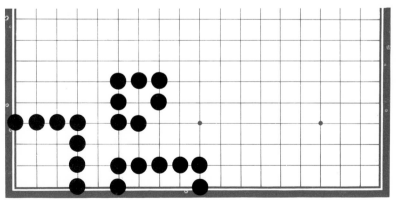

Fig. 36

played to points surrounded. This concept is of importance throughout the game, but never more so than in the opening.

If we take a seven stone army as an example, Figure 36 shows how in the centre such an army can surround only one point, on the edge three, and in the corner as many as nine points. This gives an idea why the opening struggle in Go is for control of the corners, and then the sides, the centre being the least important part of the board.

A Full-board Opening

The full-board opening shown in Figure 37 was played by two of the strongest European players, Z. Mutabzija (Jugoslavia) and H. de Vries (Holland) at the European Go Congress in Bristol in 1971. Mutabzija played Black.

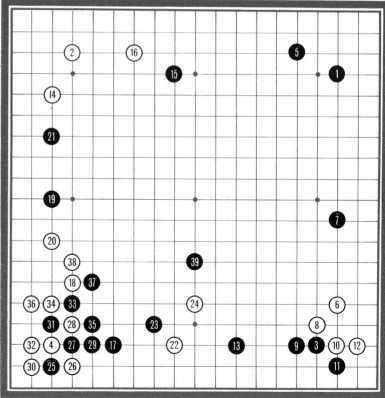

Fig. 37

Black 1 and 5, and White 2 and 14 make standard corner enclosures. Black was able to build up a wide but loose framework with his 7 and 15, the one White made with his 16 being smaller but tighter.

The sequence from 6–13 is a standard corner opening or 'joseki'. Many thousands of these have been worked out, and this one is typical, the corner being more or less evenly divided.

19 and 21 are a standard side formation. It encloses little territory, but can be fairly sure of making two eyes if required.

White 22 attacks 17 by severing it from the strong stones in the lower right corner. 23 is a strong counter attack, and 24 is defensive.

The sequence 25–38 is not standard, and in fact includes one or two doubtful moves. 25 becomes virtually dead—this stone and White 28 are deliberate sacrifices. The result is that White makes secure territory in the corner and along one side, but Black's group on the outside is very strong. Black now uses this strength together with his lower right group to mount an attack on White 22 and 24, with his 39. Now the middle game is under way.

Note how Black 39 is the first stone to pay any attention to the middle of the board—most of the opening plays are on the 3rd and 4th lines from the edge. Note also how territory is thinly sketched out at first, stones only being played next to each other when a tactical encounter develops.

Standard Corner Openings (Joseki)

The standard Japanese reference work on joseki lists some 21,000 variations. No amateur player ever comes close to knowing them all—what is more important is to understand the principles that underlie them. A few examples are given here to illustrate some of the tactical principles that apply not only in the opening but throughout the game.

The most frequently played opening move in a corner is on the '3–4' point (see Figure 38). The player's intention is to add another stone at 'a', 'b', 'c', or occasionally 'd' to make one of the standard two-stone fortifications of the corner or 'shimari'. (See the top left and top right corners of Figure 37 for examples). The best way for the opponent to challenge his hold on the corner is to attack by occupying one of these points himself.

Figure 39 shows a joseki where Black at once counter-attacks White 2 with Black 3. A move like this is called a 'squeeze' or 'pincers' attack for obvious reasons, and the idea is to stop White

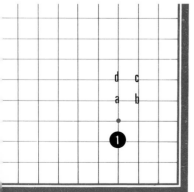

Fig. 38

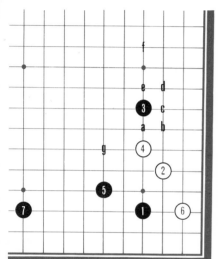

Fig. 39

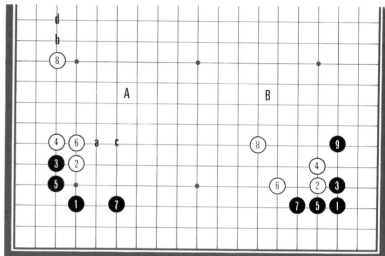

Fig. 40

from stabilizing his stone with an extension such as that between moves 19 and 21 in Figure 37. Points 'a', 'b', 'c', 'd', and 'e' are all alternative squeeze plays against White 2.

White then uses moves 4 and 6 to stabilize his stones, while Black sketches out territory with 5 and 7. Later White hopes to counter-attack Black 3 from somewhere in the region of 'f', and 'g' is also a good point for either player.

Figure 40*a* shows one of the joseki that results from White's attack at 'a' in Figure 38. Black takes territory in the corner, and White builds a strong side position.

White 8 is the optimum extension from the two stones 4 and 6. Had there been another white stone at or about 'a', the correct extension would be to 'b', and with stones at or around 'a' and 'c' the correct extension is to 'd'. In theory the opponent has no means of disconnecting such extensions. Note that they are made along the third line from the edge−extensions made in the middle of the board usually need to be somewhat closer.

Figure 40*b* shows a typical joseki resulting from an initial play on the '3−3' point. Black has taken all the corner territory, but White's stones are said to have an 'influence' towards the centre and lower edge of the board, which will be useful to him in the middle-game. White has also won the initiative from Black−now he can play first at some other important point (see also Figure 31*a*

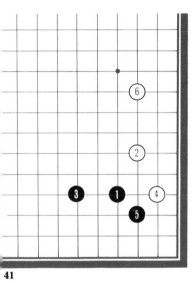

41

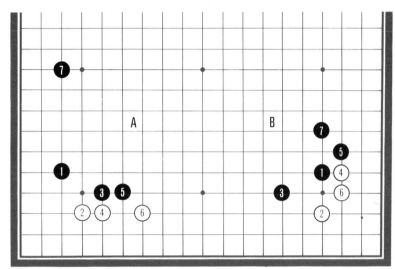

Fig. 42

for another popular '3–3' point joseki).

The other most commonly chosen opening points in the corner are the '4–4', '3–5', and '4–5' points. Figures 41, 42*a* and 42*b* respectively show a typical joseki from each opening.

Summary of Principles of Sound Play

Always consider efficiency. In the opening, sketch out territory thinly at first on the third and fourth lines from the edge, controlling first corners, then sides, lastly centre.

A move which serves several functions is always better than one with only one purpose. Never use two stones where one will do, and never play a move that gains a few points when another move elsewhere would gain more.

Always consider for each manoeuvre whether it retains or loses the initiative. Losing the initiative is not bad in itself, but only give it up for a worthwhile advantage.

Stones which could easily be linked together are hard to attack, while disconnected ones are usually an easy prey. Remember that by the end of the game all your stones are going to need to have been connected into armies that could make two eyes if needed (except in the case of the 'seki'). Don't play good stones after bad in trying to rescue stones that are virtually dead–you will only increase your loss.

Keep your options open as long as possible, e.g. which areas of territory you intend to defend, which endangered stones you are prepared to rescue, etc. Likewise, limit your opponent's options as much as possible.

Remember a one point advantage is enough to win. If you are winning, don't take chances—if losing, complicate the position.

If you are stuck for a move, imagine where your opponent would play if it were his turn. Very often your best play is at or near that point.

The Handicapping System

One of the great advantages of Go, at least from the weaker player's

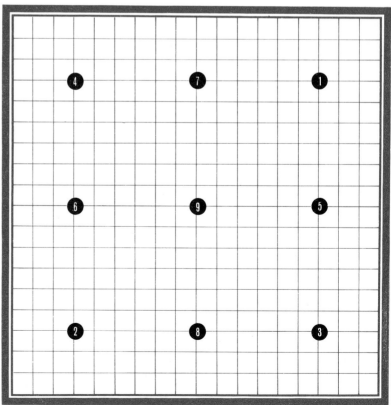

Fig. 43

point of view, is that it has a built in handicapping system, which enables two players of widely differring playing strengths to enjoy a game in which each has an equal chance of winning.

In Figure 1 you can see the nine 'handicap points', the ones marked with small dots. In a handicap game, the weaker player plays, as his first move, from two to nine stones on certain of these points to give himself just sufficient advantage to compensate for the difference in playing strengths. The handicap points are points of great strategic value and give a very considerable advantage to the Black player. The maximum normal handicap is nine stones (see Figure 43), The order of placing them shown is the traditional Japanese one.

If a player receiving a nine-stone advantage were to defeat his opponent (say) three times in succession, his opening advantage would be reduced to eight stones – the one he would lose would be the centre one (No. 9). For a seven-stone advantage stones 7 and 8 are omitted; for six stones, omit stones 7, 8, and 9; for a five-stone advantage, omit 5, 6, 7, and 8. A four stone advantage uses only stones 1, 2, 3, and 4; a three stone advantage 1, 2, and 3; two stones, 1 and 2. A 'one-stone advantage' consists of giving Black the advantage of moving first: however, this move does not have to be on a handicap point.

When players of equal strength play, it is usual to add $5\frac{1}{2}$ points to White's score at the end of the game. This compensates him for Black's advantage in moving first, and prevents a tied score.

The Grading System

All serious Go players have a grade which is somewhere on the scale shown in Figure 44. Note that the 'Kyu' (intermediate) grades are better the lower the number, whereas in the 'Dan' (master) grades the reverse applies. Handicaps are worked out according to grade, e.g. if a 2-dan player plays a 5-kyu player, the difference in grade is six (not seven, as the scale has no zero), and the 5-kyu player would play six stones on the appropriate handicap points as his first move. If a 1-dan player played a 1-kyu, the weaker player would simply have the advantage of moving first. In either case, if the players are correctly graded, each should have a 50 per cent chance of winning.

Professional players have a quite separate grading system going up to 9-dan. A professional 1-dan is about the same strength as an amateur 5-dan!

	5	GO - DAN
DAN GRADES (Master)	4	YON-DAN
	3	SAN-DAN
	2	NI-DAN
	1	SHO-DAN
	1	
	2	
	3	
	4	
KYU GRADES (Beginner and Intermediate)	5	
	6	
	7	
	8	
	9	
	10	
	11	

Fig. 44

How To Learn Go

There has only been space here for the rules and the most elementary tactics and strategy of Go. One of the great joys of the game is that while it can be played and enjoyed after ten minutes' study of the rules, if you want to take it seriously, it can occupy a lifetime of study. Professional Go players in Japan and Korea (there are about 500 of them) are apprenticed to a master player in their early teens and thereafter spend most of their waking hours playing and studying Go.

There are plenty of books in English nowadays for both the beginner and intermediate player. Advanced players have to turn to Japanese literature to some extent, but this is easier than you might think as much of the information can be gained from the diagrams, with little or no knowledge of the Japanese language.

As well as studying the literature it is necessary to play against strong players to really improve. Beginners whose only opponents are other beginners, though they may thoroughly enjoy their Go, tend to remain at a rather low playing strength. There are however plenty of opportunities to meet strong players at local Go clubs and in tournaments. In Britain it has become the tradition for even the strongest players to welcome beginners at all Go functions.

Beginners are strongly advised to start playing on the 9×9 board, then to progress to the intermediate 13×13 board, and to delay tackling the 19×19 board until they have really understood the basic tactics of Go. One really does learn more soundly this way.

Go is rooted in the culture of China, Korea and Japan and followed with a fervour accorded to no comparable Western game. (There are eight million players in Japan alone.) Two World Chess Champions, Bobby Fischer and Emmanuel Lasker, have been Go players, and the latter's namesake Dr. Edward Lasker (the author of a book on Go), predicted that Go would eventually replace chess as the leading intellectual game of the West, and that Western Go players would eventually rival the top Oriental players. Only time will prove him right or wrong, but Go is certainly here to stay!

Hex

Hex is a board game of pure skill for two players. Its rules are very simple, but it is a game of considerable interest, and deserving of more attention than it has yet received.

Hex is played on a diamond shaped board ruled into equilateral triangles, the standard size board having ten triangles along each edge (see Figure 1). Play takes place on the points of intersection of the lines as in Go, and not within the triangles.

Algebraic notation is used to define points, and for this purpose vertical lines are ignored. Thus the central point is referred to as F6, and not F11 or L6.

Moves are also made as in Go—starting with the board empty players alternately place men on any vacant point, Black moving first. Once played men are not moved, and there is no capturing.

Each player's object is to build a continuous chain of adjacent men linking any point on one of the sides marked with his colour

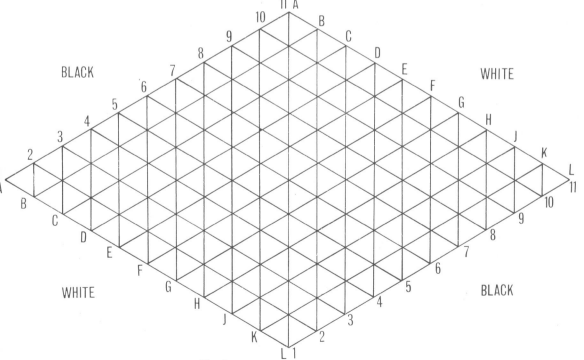

Fig. 1

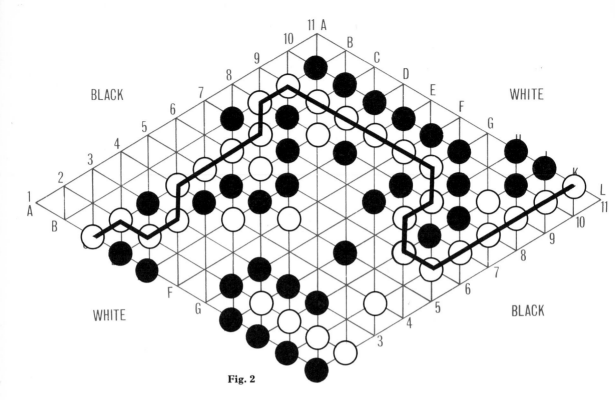

Fig. 2

to any point on the opposite side. Corner points may be used by either player to reach his side.

Figure 2 shows the end of a game of hex which White has won. The heavy black line picks out the continuous chain of men with which he has linked his two sides. Note that a winning chain can turn and double back as much as it likes as long as it has no gaps. Notice also that a game of hex cannot be drawn. There is no way Black could now connect his two sides without the chain crossing the white one somewhere.

We will now examine the game which ended as in Figure 2. You are advised to play the moves through on a board.

Moves 1–20 (see Figure 3)

Black 1: The strongest opening move is on the centre point—however, as this gives Black a considerable advantage it is customary to bar opening there, or sometimes on the entire short diagonal. The latter rule was in force in this game.

White 2: A typical reply.

Black 3: This makes a 'double connection'—the two black men cannot be disconnected because as soon as White plays F7 or F8 Black plays the other.

White 4: Tries to block Black 3 from the lower right side.

Black 5–White 9: More double connections by Black, and more blocks by White. Black has a rather inflexible position, but White has a weak point at K5.

Black 9–Black 15: Black cuts White off from the lower left side, and the following plays look rather submissive on Black's part. However, he is being chased in the direction he wants to go (towards A1), so

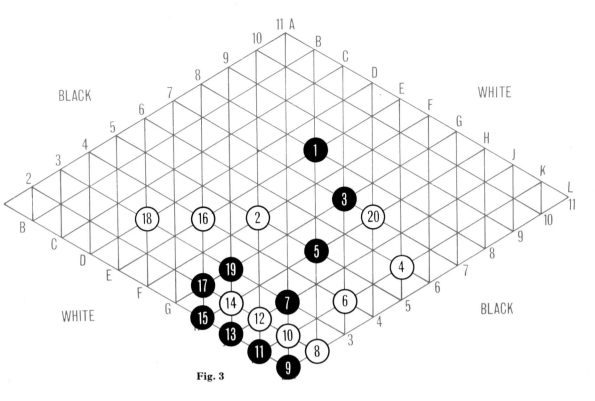

Fig. 3

Black is happy knowing that White cannot keep this up too long.
White 16 : This man threatens to connect both to the lower left side and to White 14.
Black 17 : Threatens to break both these connections, so;
White 18 : Preserves the possibility of connecting to the lower left side, and hints at a possible winning chain via the C9 area.
Black 19 : Carrying out the threat to disconnect 14 from 16.
White 20 : A subtle move, threatening to link the white men (and therefore disconnect the black ones) with a play at H4. Without White 20 Black could parry this threat by disconnecting White at his weak point of K5 e.g. White H4, Black K5, White H6, Black G6, White J5, Black H7, White J6, Black J8, etc. However, White 20 protects this weakness at K5.

Moves 21–40 (see Figure 4)

Black 21 : A very solid reply.
White 22 : He has to play somewhere in this area as Black 1 is now potentially connected, via double connections and directly, to L1 on the lower right side, and he must therefore disconnect it from the upper left side.
Black 23 : Trying to block White 22 from the upper right side, but;
White 24–White 34 : In a forced sequence White connects his 22 to the upper right side using his 20 and 4 on the way. Of course the chain still has some gaps, but these are all of the 'double connection' variety, so Black has no way to break through.
Black 35–White 36 : Black's only hope is to push through between White 2 and 22, and White's defensive block at a distance is usually the right way to handle such a frontal assault.

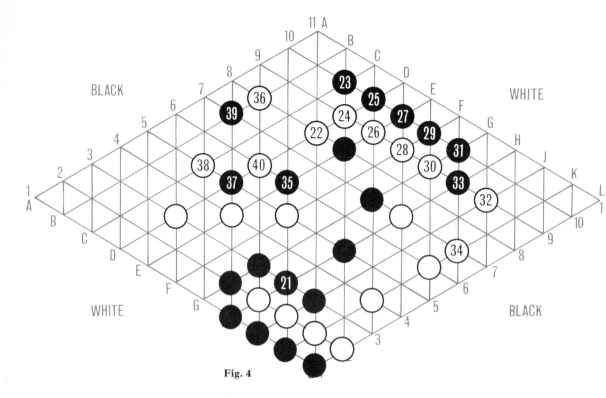

Fig. 4

Black 37–White 38: White is prepared to abandon his 2 and 16. He doesn't mind which way his winning chain runs!
Black 39: An attempt to confuse the situation.
White 40: Probably best, but . . .

Moves 41–68 (see Figure 5)

Black missed a chance to win with 41 D4. After missing this chance, the game goes downhill for him – he plays his remaining moves only in the hope of a mistake by White.

After White 44 he threatens a double connection with the upper right side with B10 or A11. Black 45 prevents this, but White just plays 46 and uses the connection he established with moves 24–34. White 50 and 52 are standard replies to an attempt to break a double connection to a side point. The remaining moves are trivial as they consist of threats to break double connections and their replies.

As in most games of strategy, it pays in hex to keep your options open as long as possible. Black lost this game because of a too solid style of play, especially in over-reliance on the double connection in the opening stages.

Hex was invented in Denmark in the 1940s and enjoyed a brief vogue there and subsequent pockets of interest in the U.S.A. However, there is almost no literature on the game, and at the time of writing the game is not manufactured. It is however quite easy to make a board and to use Go stones or counters for the men, or you can play with a pencil on isometric drawing paper.

Some players prefer a board drawn as a tesselation of hexagons, playing inside the hexagons instead of on the intersections as in the version shown here. The game comes to the same thing, but

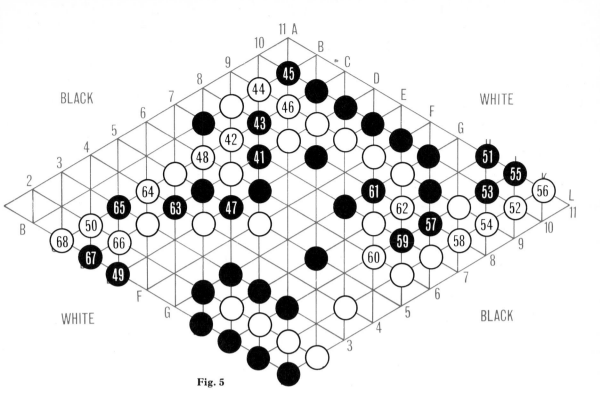

Fig. 5

the board is far harder to draw!

Other size boards than the one shown may be used. I think that as the game comes to be studied more larger boards may well be used.

The lack of hex literature is an advantage for the player who likes a game that depends mainly on over-the-board ability rather than prior book study. It is of course an irony of this and all such games that as general interest in it grows, so also will the amount of book work required to become a stronger player.

Reversi

Reversi is a board game for two using an ordinary draughtsboard (chequerboard) and 64 identical men similar to draughtsmen with the two sides of each man in contrasting colours usually, as here, black and red.

The game was invented in England in the late nineteenth century when it became briefly popular. It continues to enjoy a modest following but should be better known as it is skilful and fast-moving with dramatic changes of fortune and is also a good family game.

Many variations of Reversi have been tried (for example, on different size boards) but the version given here is the standard one. Cheap sets are readily obtainable but the men may easily be improvised.

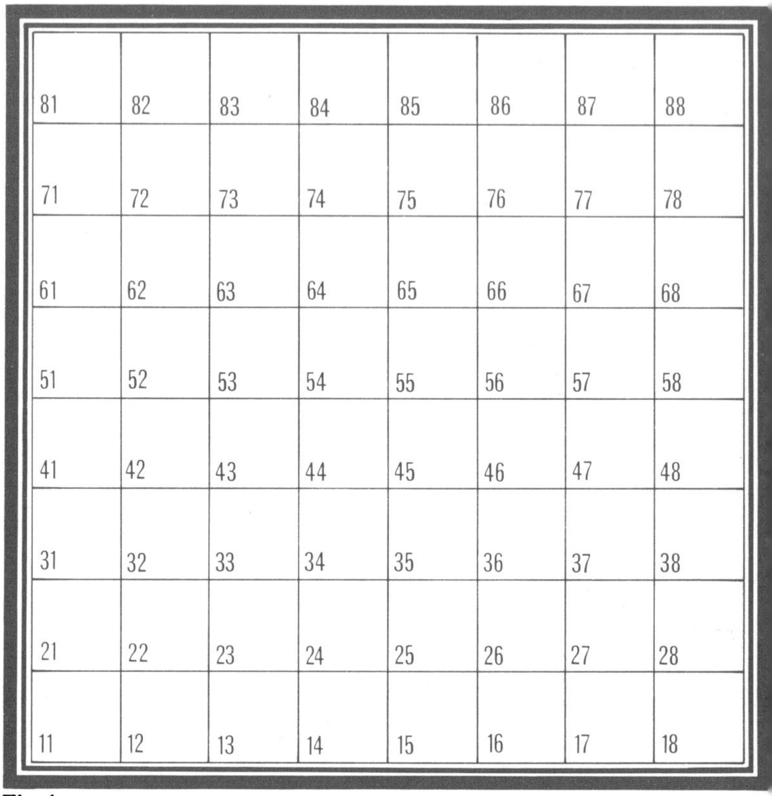

81	82	83	84	85	86	87	88
71	72	73	74	75	76	77	78
61	62	63	64	65	66	67	68
51	52	53	54	55	56	57	58
41	42	43	44	45	46	47	48
31	32	33	34	35	36	37	38
21	22	23	24	25	26	27	28
11	12	13	14	15	16	17	18

Fig. 1

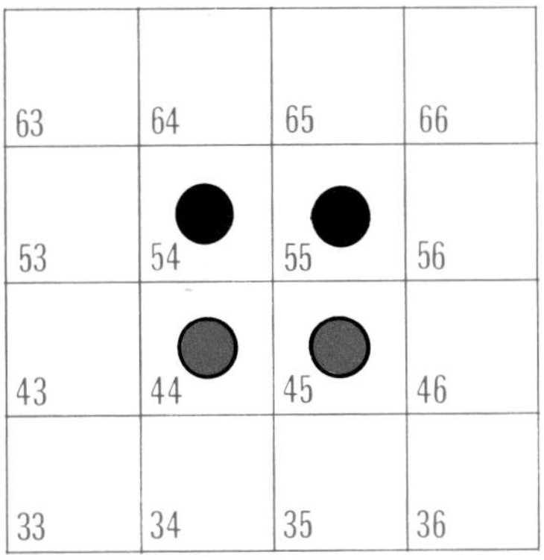

Fig. 2

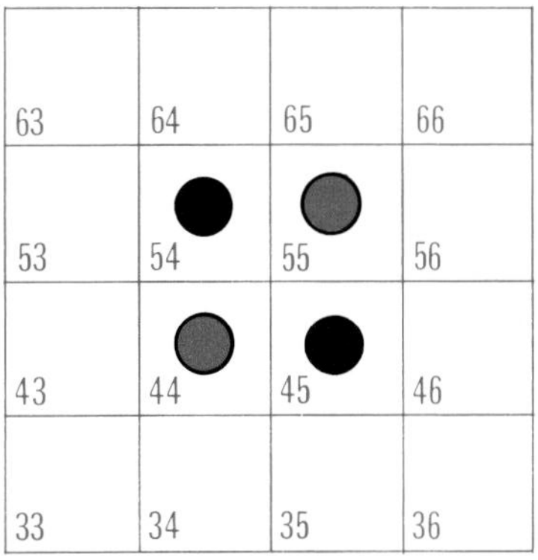

Fig. 3

Preparation for Play

Players toss for colour then each takes 32 men and arranges them in front of him, own colour uppermost.

The board is placed between the players without regard to orientation as the colours of the squares have no significance in the game.

Before we go further it is necessary to annotate the board for reference. An adequate notation is shown in Figure 1 with the colours of the squares omitted for clarity. It will be seen that each row (rank) is numbered progressively up the board in tens, and each column (file) progressively from left to right in units.

The board is now dressed by the players alternately placing two men, one at a time, on the four central squares. Clearly only two arrangements are possible, with like men either side-by-side (Figure 2, preferred by experts) or diagonally opposite (Figure 3).

Play

Red plays first and places a man on any vacant square orthogonally or diagonally adjacent to a square already occupied by a black man such that the black man is flanked by two red men. It can be readily seen that Red has four, and only four legal plays in either of the two initial arrangements. When a man has been trapped in this manner it is reversed to show the colour of its captor. For example, if the board were dressed diagonally (black men on 45 and 54), and Red played first on 35, the black man on 45 would be turned over, when there would be four red men on the board and only one black man (on 54).

Now it is Black to play and he can occupy 34, 36 or 56, reversing one red man in each case.

Object of the Game

The object of the game is to have a majority of your colour on the board at the end. Play ceases when all the squares have been filled or when neither player has a legal move (i.e., cannot make a capture). If at any time one player is unable to move, he misses his turn.

Strategy

As the board fills up from the centre, opportunities will occur to capture several men in a single play. Men captured are determined solely by the last piece played, when every enemy man in an unbroken line between it and the next friendly man *in any and every*

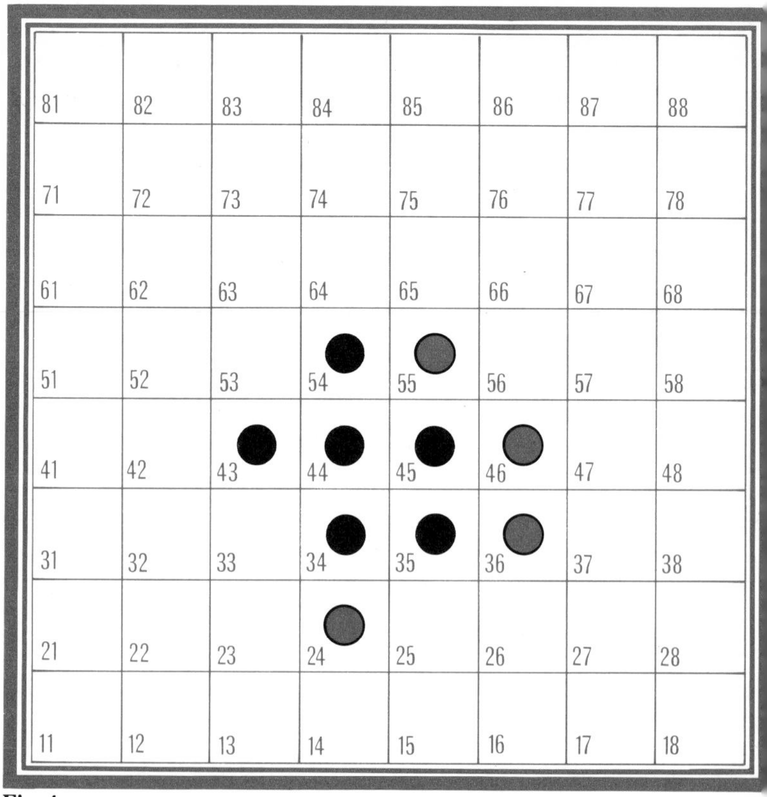

Fig. 4

direction are captured and reversed. Theoretically, as many as 1[?] men can change sides in one play though about half this number i[?] the usual maximum.

Figure 4 shows a game in progress with Red to move. In thi[?] position, Red has five plays:

25 – reversing the two men on 35 and 45
33 – reversing the two men on 34 and 35 and the man on 44
42 – reversing the three men on 43, 44 and 45
53 – reversing the man on 54
64 – reversing the men on 34, 44 and 54

Remember that the man played alone dictates the men captured[?] Thus if Red here plays 33, then after reversal of 34, 35 and 44 th[?] black man on 45, although surrounded, is not reversed.

All captured men must be reversed at once but there is n[?] requirement to make the numerically largest capture.

Notice that if there is a gap anywhere in a line of men flanked b[?] two men of the opposite colour, either between the men in th[?] line or between one of the end men and a flanking man, then non[?] of the men is reversed. Similarly, a line of men cannot be trapped i[?] one of them is on the board edge as then it is impossible to satisf[?] the conditions of capture. However, if the line runs along the boar[?] edge, then the men can be captured unless a corner square i[?] occupied by one of the group when capture again becomes impos-sible.

It will be seen from this that certain squares can be more valuabl[?] than others. Figure 5 identifies best squares to occupy (white[?] and worse (red) with shading showing relative values of the others[?]

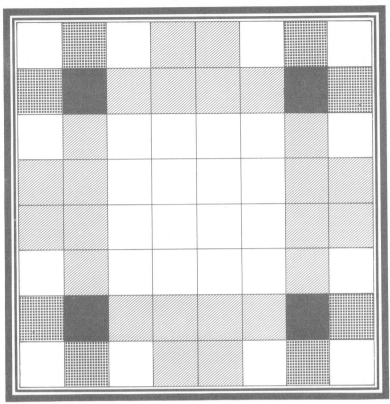

Fig. 5

It will be seen that the four squares diagonally in from the corners are especially to be avoided because their occupancy is likely to allow the opponent into the strong corners securing all adjacent men in three directions.

'This is only a relative guide however, useful as all such guides are useful, but not to be followed slavishly as positions can often arise where square values may vary from those shown.

The concept of key squares nevertheless remains at the root of Reversi strategy and it is usually better to forgo the capture of, say, five men, if an important square can be gained for, say, the capture of only two or three men.

Generally speaking, one should aim at filling in the centre before expanding outwards to the sides (notice in Figure 5 that the 12 squares that surround the four dressed squares in the centre are all classed as valuable).

It is not easy to see ahead accurately more than a move or two in Reversi except in the closing stages of a game, but with practice one can develop a feel for good and bad formations – and unlike so many games, Reversi, because of its fluctuating fortunes, can never be dull.

Wari

There is a whole family of games, commonly referred to generically as Mancala, whose common features are that they are games of skill, usually for two players, in which a number of stones or beans initially distributed among two, three or four rows of cups, are redistributed or 'sown' according to certain rules; contents of cups are captured from time to time by one or other of the players the winner being the player who acquires more than half of the available stones.

Mancala has been described as the national game of Africa and has a good claim to being the oldest board game extant as it is believed to have been popular during the Empire Age of Ancient Egypt well over 3,000 years ago. There are at least two hundred recorded regional variants of Mancala, each with its own local name. One of the most widely played is Wari, originating in West Africa where the 'boards' are often simply holes scooped out of the ground (though boards are also carved from wood, often elaborately) with the 'stones' usually beans, pebbles or shells.

A Wari board consists of 12 cups arranged in two parallel rows of six with a large cup at each end, one for each player, to keep prisoners (Figure 1).

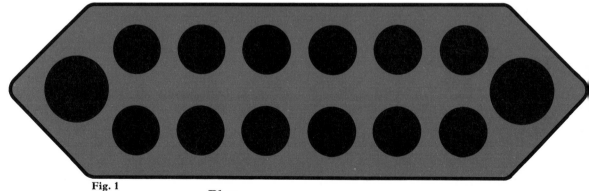

Fig. 1

Play

The two players face each other across the board which is placed lengthways between them, each player assuming control of the row of six cups nearest to him.

The board is dressed by placing four stones in each of the 12 cups, there being no differentiation between the stones of the two sides.

The players decide who shall start, and the first player lifts *all*

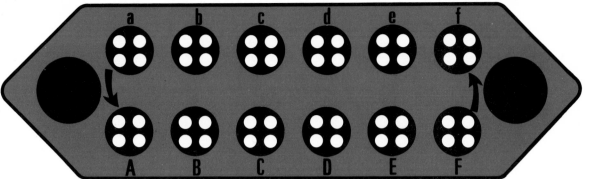

Fig. 2

the stones from any cup of his choice *on his side of the board* and sows the stones one at a time into successive cups in an anti-clockwise direction starting with the cup immediately to the right of the emptied cup and continuing round his opponents cups if necessary. The second player then takes all the stones from one of the cups on *his* side of the board (4 or 5 as the case may be) and sows them similarly, still in an anti-clockwise direction.

Play continues in this way until one player puts the *last* stone from one of his cups into an opponent's cup that contains *one* or *two* stones (i.e., two or three stones after distribution has been completed). The player is entitled to all the stones in this cup as prisoners. He scoops them out and puts them in his large hole at the end of the rows. If there are also precisely two or three stones in the *preceding* cup, and this cup is also on the opponent's side, then these stones too are taken prisoner. Similarly with the next cup. If any cup has less than two or more than three stones in it, however, then these stones are immune from capture as are the stones of any cups which preceded it in the distribution, regardless of their contents. Some simple examples will serve to explain these points.

Let us call the players White and Black, and annotate the cups on White's side A–F and those on Black's side a–f, from left to right looked at from White's side in each case. The starting position is then as shown in Figure 2. The arrows indicate direction of play.

Supposing White starts and elects to pick up the stones in cup E. He must pick up *all* the stones. He then sows them anti-clockwise, dropping the first stone in F, the second in f, the third in e and the fourth in d. As d does not now contain either two or three stones, no captures are made and the turn ends. We can record this simply as E(4), the letter indicating the cup emptied and the number of stones in it. There is no need to indicate the player, as each can only empty a cup on his own side of the board and can only capture stones on his opponent's side. Let us continue a move or two: f(5); B(4); a(5)

The position is now as shown in Figure 3. Black's last play was into cup E which now has two stones in it. Accordingly, these stones are removed and are now Black's prisoners. If D had had 2 or 3 stones in it, Black would have captured these as well. If each of the cups A–E had had either 2 or 3 stones in them after the distribution from a, then Black would have taken the contents of all these cups.

There are only a few other rules. If a cup contains more than 11 stones and hence at least one circuit of the board is completed, the

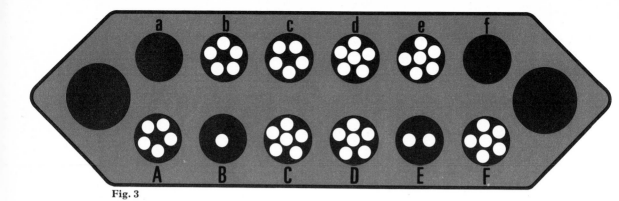

Fig. 3

cup from which the stones were lifted must remain empty. Thus if 12 stones were distributed, the last stone would be dropped into the cup immediately beyond the starting cup.

A player may not empty or leave empty *all* the cups on his opponent's side. He must play so as to leave at least one stone for his opponent to sow (it is hard to find a parallel of this compassionate rule in European games). If he is unable to do so, he (the player) takes all the stones remaining (which must perforce be on his side of the board) and adds them to his prisoners and the game is over.

Sometimes in the late stages of a game a position arises where no further meaningful plays are possible (for example, if White has only one stone left at C and Black only one stone left at c, these two stones will simply follow each other round). In this case, the players take up the stones on their respective sides of the board and the game is over.

Hints on Play

There is no chance in Wari, so theoretically a 'best play' can be calculated in any position. In practice, of course, the possibilities to be considered are astronomical except in the late stages of a game, so precise computation is out of the question.

Simple tactics become evident after a game or two. For example, a cup containing two stones is obviously vulnerable to an enemy cup that contains the correct number of stones to reach it. The weakness can be defended by (a) emptying a cup that will allow a stone to be added to the two thus making that cup impregnable; or (b) playing so as to add a stone to the enemy cup so that it will overshoot its target; or (c) emptying the cup and distributing the two stones. This last is not usually satisfactory as the second player has only to feed one stone into the empty cup to make it vulnerable again.

An aggressive game calls for a build-up in your right-hand cups. If the number of stones in any cup is such that the last stone in that cup will be sown in home territory, then clearly that cup is inoffensive and the stones in it poorly deployed. Aim to get several of the opponent's cups simultaneously under attack.

Mah Jong

Mah Jong is a game for four players (two- and three-player versions exist but are unsatisfactory). Mah Jong has affinities to the card game, Rummy, and like that game, the element of luck is considerable while still leaving scope for skilful play.

Mah Jong in its present form is probably about a hundred years old, a development of early Chinese card and domino games, themselves derived from ancient Chinese paper money. Mah Jong cards (narrow strips of pasteboard) are still used, but the game is commonly played with tiles, once made of ivory or bone and often backed with wood, particularly bamboo, but now almost invariably manufactured of plastic.

The game is widely played today throughout the Far East and among Chinese communities everywhere. One of the distinctive sounds in the back streets of Singapore and Hong Kong is the audible shuffling of the tiles–'the twittering of the sparrows'.

Mah Jong was first introduced to the West as a card game before the turn of the century but it was not until after the First World War, when it reappeared in its present form, that it acquired any popularity. The Mah Jong craze of the 1920s, particularly evident in America, soon passed, a victim of proliferating rules and the rising appeal of Contract Bridge.

Rules

There are two basic games; the uncomplicated Mah Jong of the East, essentially a gambling game, and the Western version which has many 'special hands', more elaborate scoring and sometimes extra tiles. Although a number of attempts have been made to codify Mah Jong, there are no universally acknowledged rules, certainly for the Western game, though the version offered here, a compromise between the two extremes, has achieved wide acceptance. Nevertheless, rules should always be agreed before play to avoid misunderstandings.

Equipment

Tiles. A modern set comprises 136 tiles of which 108 are 'suit' tiles and 28 are 'honour' tiles.

There are three suits in Mah Jong; Bamboos (commonly called 'sticks'), Characters (sometimes called 'numbers') and Circles ('dots'). There are 36 tiles in each suit, four of each number from one to nine.

The honour tiles consist of four each of Winds (East, South,

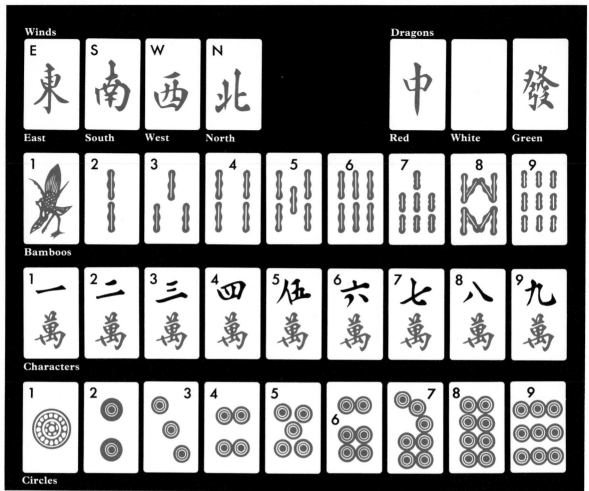

Fig. 1

West and North) and Dragons (Red, Green and White). The reverse side of all tiles is uniform, invariably plain. The 34 different values are shown in Figure 1. Notice that the ones and nines of each suit are known as terminals.

A few sets also have decorative tiles known as Flowers and Seasons, each tile different and numbered. These earn bonus points but otherwise have no part in the play and these days they are little used.

Bones. These are really counters or chips, but are long and thin with the value of each stamped on it. Common denominations are 10, 100 and 500.

Dice. Two conventional dice are used in the preliminaries.

Wind Disc. This is simply a marker to show 'prevailing wind' (i.e., the dealer).

Racks. Sets often include racks to hold the hands of each player. Tiles can also be stood on end, blank side facing the other players, or held in the palm of the hand.

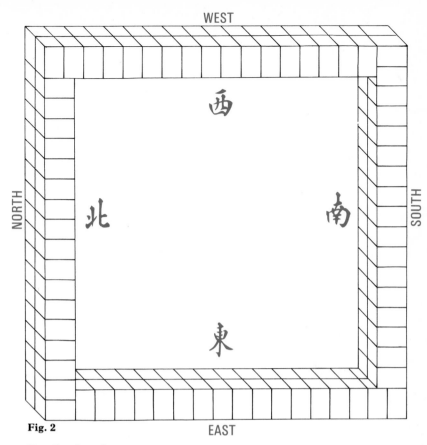

Fig. 2

WEST

NORTH

SOUTH

EAST

Preliminaries

Few games can have such elaborate preliminaries as Mah Jong. Some enthusiasts consider these add flavour to the game.

1) One player takes one each of the wind tiles and shuffles them face down. Each player then picks up a tile, the shuffler taking the last one. East is first dealer, who chooses his seat. South sits on his right, North on his left and West opposite him. Note that this does not correspond to our arrangement of the compass points.

2) The 136 tiles are now mixed face down with all players taking part in the shuffling. Each player then builds a wall 17 tiles long and 2 high, all tiles face down. When the walls are complete they are moved together to form a hollow square. This is the Great Wall of China, secured against demons (Figure 2).

3) The dealer (East Wind) now throws the dice, adds the two numbers together and counts round the walls *anti-clockwise*, beginning with his own. Thus if East threw a 2 and a 5, totalling seven, he would count 'East 1, South 2, West 3, North 4, East 5, South 6, West 7'. To determine the point at which the wall will be broken, West (or whichever player at whom the count ended) then throws the dice and adds the total to that of East's throw. If West threw two 3's, for example, making 13 in all, West would then start counting along the tiles of his wall *from right to left*, breaking the wall between the 13th and 14th tiles. (If West had thrown a double 6, making a total of 19, he would have continued counting round the corner onto South's side.)

4) The players now draw their hands from the wall in the following manner. East, as dealer, first takes the four tiles (two stacks of two)

immediately beyond the break. Each of the other players do likewise in turn (South, West, North), the wall thus being dismantled clockwise. This procedure is repeated three times when each player has twelve tiles. East then takes the next two tiles and the other players in turn take one more each from the wall, always the tile nearest the break and top before bottom. The hands, which are concealed from the other players, are now complete and play can start.

Object of the Game

The aim of each player is to make the highest score which is usually synonomous with being the first to go Mah Jong (go out), similar to Rummy. A player may go out when he has arranged his hand into four sets and a pair, or completes a special hand (see below).

There are three kinds of sets:

1) A sequence (CHOW); any three consecutive tiles of the same suit
2) A triplet (PUNG); any three identical suit or honour tiles
3) A four (KONG); any four identical suit or honour tiles.

A pair is any two identical tiles.

In the hand shown in Figure 3, the player is waiting for a North Wind or an 8 of Characters to go out.

Play

1) Dealer starts by discarding a tile of his choice face up inside the wall. All players now hold 13 tiles. Dealer's subsequent discards are laid face up in a continuous row so that the other players can see what he has discarded and in what order. The other players follow the same procedure. An alternative system is for discards to be placed face up at random within the wall.

2) After the dealer has discarded, and assuming no other player wants his discard (see below), play will continue anti-clockwise. South will take the next tile from the wall (at the point where North removed the last tile for his hand), discarding at will, and so on until a player goes Mah Jong, or Wu as it is sometimes called.

3) A set can be made in two ways:

a) It can be picked up in the initial hand, or drawn from the wall, or a combination of these. This is known as a *concealed* Chow, Pung or Kong.

b) It can be completed by picking up the third tile (or fourth in the case of a Kong) discarded by another player. This is known as an

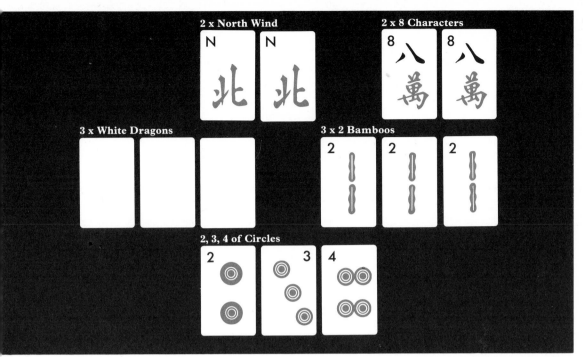

2 x North Wind

2 x 8 Characters

3 x White Dragons

3 x 2 Bamboos

2, 3, 4 of Circles

Fig. 3

exposed or open Chow, Pung or Kong. (An exposed Kong can also be obtained by adding a tile drawn from the wall to an exposed Pung but not by claiming a discard to add to an exposed Pung.)

4) Concealed sets (except Kongs, see below) are not disclosed until the end of play. They are worth double exposed sets (except Chows). Exposed sets are placed face up in front of the owner, between the rack and the wall.

5) Only the discard of the last player can be claimed, and that before the next player has picked up a tile. Only the next player in sequence can claim a discard to complete a Chow, but any player can claim a discard to complete a Pung or a Kong or to go Mah Jong (completing a set *or* the necessary pair to go out). The player or players requiring the discard shout 'Chow', 'Pung', 'Kong' or 'Wu', as appropriate. Precedence is in ascending order of value, with a player claiming a Chow having lowest priority and a player calling Wu, highest. Where more than one player is claiming Wu, the player first in rotation of play has prior right.

6) A player who wins a discard takes the tile into his hand and *at once* completes a set, which is then exposed, or goes out. If he does not go out, he must himself discard before completing his turn. A discard may not be claimed to keep in hand nor to add to an exposed Pung. The turn of play then passes to the player immediately to the right of the player claiming the discard. Thus if East throws away and North legally claims the discard, then play will again pass to East; South and West having effectively lost their turns.

7) A special procedure occurs when a player completes a Kong. If this is picked up in the initial hand, then the player must wait until his turn when he declares it, placing it on the table, the two central tiles face up and the outside tiles face down to show that it is a concealed set. He then draws a tile from the wall *but does not*

discard. If a player completes a concealed Kong during play and claims it, or claims a discard to make an exposed Kong, or draws the fourth tile to add to an exposed Pung, he must draw a further tile from the wall and discard in the usual way when his turn ends. This procedure is designed to ensure that the right number of tiles are always in hand to go Mah Jong (four sets and a pair). A player with an exposed Pung may hold the fourth tile in his hand but elect not to complete the Kong (because, for instance, he wants the fourth tile for a Chow). In this case he cannot claim points for a Kong if another player goes Wu, nor can he draw another tile. He may subsequently, however, decide to convert his Pung into a Kong when he follows the procedure set out above.

8) If nobody has gone Mah Jong when the wall has been reduced to 14 tiles (the 'dead wall', often separated slightly from the main wall at start of play), the game is abandoned without scoring.

Scoring
Scoring, like the preliminaries, can be complicated. First, the winner (the player to go out) adds up his points as below.

Scoring Table

Points awarded for	Amount scored
–going Mah Jong	20
–going Mah Jong and drawing last tile from wall (i.e., not a discard)	2
–going Mah Jong with the last tile from the wall (excluding the 14 dead tiles)	2
–an exposed Pung of	
simple tiles (2–8)	2
terminal tiles (1, 9)	4
honour tiles	4
–an exposed Kong of	
simple tiles	8
terminal tiles	16
honour tiles	16

Concealed Pungs and Kongs count DOUBLE.
Chows score NOTHING, whether concealed or exposed.
Pairs score as follows:

Dragons	2
Dealer's (prevailing) wind	2
One's own wind	2

Notice in particular that Chows earn nothing while Pungs and Kongs of terminals earn the same as honour tiles, and concealed sets are worth double exposed sets. Certain pairs can also earn points, as shown. They score the same whether the pair was concealed or completed from a discard to go out. Some schools allow a number of additional bonuses but these are omitted in this description for simplicity.

When the points are added, they are *doubled* for *every time* that the following conditions can be satisfied:
1) Holding a Pung or Kong of:
a) Dragons
b) Dealer's (prevailing) Wind
c) Own Wind
2) The tile to go out is drawn from the wall
3) The tile to go out is the last tile of the wall (excluding the 14 dead tiles)
4) The hand is all of one suit with Winds or Dragons
5) The hand is all Pungs

They are *doubled twice* whenever the hand contains a triplet or four of the player's wind *when he is dealer* and *doubled four times* when the player's hand is all of the same suit or all terminals or all honours tiles.

Payment
Only the player who goes Mah Jong scores his hand. The other players each pay him the total score, rounded up to the nearest ten. The dealer (prevailing wind) pays *double*, but if he is the player who goes Mah Jong all the other players pay him double.

Some players score every hand, each player settling the difference between his score and those of the other players, but this is very confusing and is not recommended.

It is usual to agree a limit score for a hand. This is usually 500.

Example of Scoring
East is dealer and goes Mah Jong, drawing his last tile from the wall, with the following hand:
    Concealed Kong of East Wind
    Exposed Pung of Red Dragons
    Concealed Pung of 1 Circles
    Concealed Chow (3, 4, 5 of Bamboos)
    Pair of Green Dragons

He scores:

Going Mah Jong	20
Drawing last tile from wall	2
Concealed Kong of East Wind	32
Exposed Pung of Red Dragons	4
Concealed Pung of 1 Circles	8
Concealed Chow	0
Pair of Green Dragons	2
	68

He doubles his hand once for:
Pung of Dragons
Going out with tile from the wall
He doubles his hand *twice* for:
Kong of dealer's wind when dealer
The hand thus earns four doubles, making a total well in excess of the limit hand, hence the total score for payment is 500. But East is dealer, so each of the other players must pay him 1,000 points. There are no other payments.

Special Hands

Many consider that Mah Jong was suffocated by the proliferation of 'special hands' introduced from time to time 'to make the game more interesting'. However, certain of these hands, including one or two admitted in the Chinese game, have achieved general acceptance and are given below. They are all 'limit' hands.

1) *Concealed Triplets* Four Pungs and a pair, ALL tiles drawn from the wall. Sometimes Kongs, if concealed, are also allowed in this hand.
2) *Four Big Winds* Four sets of Winds plus a pair.
3) *The Snake* 1−9 of a suit plus one of each of the Winds with any tile paired. All tiles except the last must be drawn from the wall.
4) *Heavenly Hand* (Dealer only) Go Mah Jong with the 14 tiles dealt; i.e., without any play taking place.
5) *The Gates of Heaven* A Pung of 1's, a Pung of 9's, and one each of the tiles 2−8, one of them doubled and all tiles of the same suit.
6) *All Pair Honour Hand* 7 pairs of honour and/or terminal tiles.

Hints on Play

It is necessary to strike a balance between building a high-score hand and going Mah Jong as soon as possible. The dealer (whose awards and penalties are doubled) should always strive to go out.

As with Rummy, discards can be important indicators of opponents' hands – watch them.

It is always advisable to monitor the pool of dead tiles – it is not much use waiting for a second Green Dragon to complete your pair if three have been discarded!

An open-ended consecutive suit pair – say, 4 and 5 of Circles – obviously offers better chances of a Chow than a pair with only one end open (say, 1 and 2) or a split pair (6 and 8).

Defer the discard of a tile you think may be wanted – particularly the dealer's wind.

Be alert for the tiles you want – a good player plays quickly to prevent the other players claiming discards.

If a game has been going on for some time, strive to go out rather than trying to improve your hand – other players are likely to be near Mah Jong. Most winning hands, unlike the example given above, are low-scoring.

Dominoes

Dominoes, like playing cards, are not a game but a whole family of games of varying complexity and suitable for almost any number of players.

The history of dominoes is obscure but they likely came from China where they have been in use for many hundreds of years. It is interesting that Chinese dominoes and playing cards are virtually indistinguishable. The origin of the name is also clouded and there are several theories, but none of them is particularly convincing.

Domino games are generally simpler than other games in this book because their scope is more limited but it is nevertheless possible to develop considerable skill in play.

Most games of dominoes are played with a double-six pack which consists of 28 tiles (see Figure 1). The tiles themselves are black or white with the spots–known as 'pips'–in a contrasting colour, usually white or black respectively. Each tile is divided into two, each half representing a number between 0 (blank) and 6. Notice that if the blanks are excluded the other tiles correspond to every possible combination of the throws of two dice. One can consider the single blank tiles as the throws of a single die with the double-blank to complete the set. (There are no blanks in the Chinese pack.)

Double-nine and double-twelve packs are used in some multi-player games but are not discussed here as these packs are not seen very often.

Certain procedures are common to all or most domino games:
1) The pack is first shuffled face down, all the players taking part.
2) Players each draw a domino from the pack to determine first lead. Highest double takes precedence, or if there are no doubles, highest domino (total pips). Tiles are again shuffled before play, which is clockwise.
3) A number of dominoes are now drawn by each player, the manner of dealing and the numbers taken depending on the game. Tiles in hand are concealed from the other players.
4) In almost all games, players take it in turns to put a domino face up on the table; second and subsequent dominoes are joined to form one continuous chain or 'leg' with pips matching on adjacent dominoes and with doubles placed at right angles to the leg. Thus there are two open ends to a domino chain which can be conveniently made to turn corners to keep the playing area manageable.

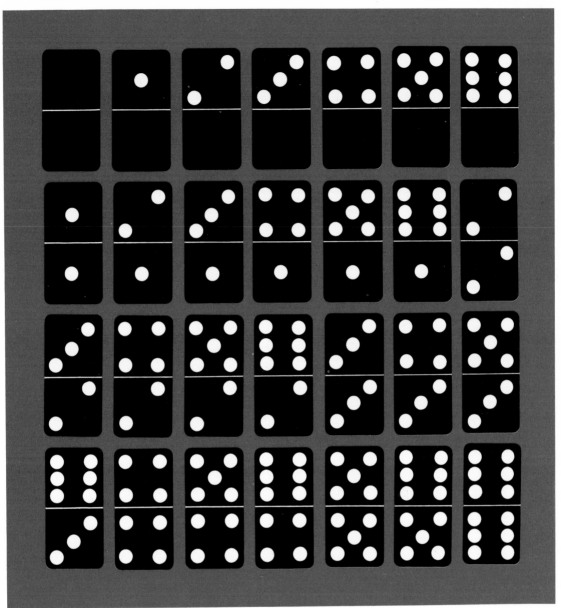

Fig. 1

5) When a player cannot match from hand either of the dominoes at the ends of the chain, he is blocked and signifies this by knocking on the table. In some games he may draw a tile from the stock, or 'boneyard' as it is usually called, or receive one from another player, but otherwise misses his turn.

6) The object of most games is to be the first to go out—i.e., get rid of all one's tiles—but in some games this is secondary to making scoring plays.

7) Partnerships are usual in four-player games. Partners sit opposite each other as in Bridge.

8) The score may be kept on paper but a cribbage board is often used for this purpose, particularly in pub games and it has the advantage of allowing all players to see easily the state of the score.

117

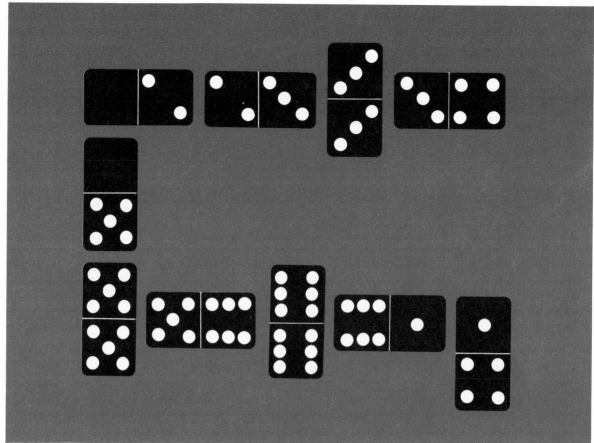

Fig. 2

The Block Game

The Block Game can be played by two, three or four players (in partnership), and is probably the most widely played of all domino games.

Preparation for the two-player variant is as above. Each player takes seven dominoes from the boneyard into hand. The holder of the highest double plays first by placing it in the centre of the table. If neither player holds a double the tiles are reshuffled.

The second player places a domino, one end of which must match the 'starter', with this end against the double but at right angles to it. The first player on his second turn has a choice between placing a matching domino against the starter or against the end of the second player's domino. Play continues in this fashion, doubles always being placed at right angles to the leg. A player who is unable to play must pass his turn. If both players are unable to add to the leg, the hand ends; the player with the smaller total number of pips on the tiles remaining in his hand is the winner and he scores the difference between this total and the total of his opponent's pips. If one player goes out (or 'domino') he scores the total of his opponent's remaining tiles. Thus if A goes out and B has the 6–3 and 4–1 left, A scores 14. A game is played to an agreed total—50 or 100 is common.

Each player also draws seven tiles in the three- and four-player variants. In the latter, all the dominoes are in play so the hand must be started with a double 6. The hand ends when *one* player goes out; the partnership scoring the total pips of the opponents' dominoes *less* the pips of the remaining partner.

Figure 2 shows a two-handed Block game in progress. Play was started with a double-6. Both ends of the leg are 4-spots so only a domino with a 4-spot can be played. Half the dominoes are, of course, out of play in the boneyard.

The Draw Game

This is very similar to the Block Game except that the starter may be any domino and a player may, on his turn, *whether he can add to the leg or not* draw one or more dominoes from the boneyard *except that the last two may not be touched*. Thus if player A in a two-player Draw Game puts down the 5–4, B may elect to draw a tile from the boneyard. He can then put down a domino or draw another tile from the boneyard, and so on. Only when a player has drawn *all* the remaining tiles in the boneyard (except the last two) can he pass. Thus if B cannot play to the leg and there are three tiles in the boneyard he must draw one tile and must play this tile if he can do so, otherwise he may pass. In the four-player version, players draw only six dominoes each at the start, leaving four in the boneyard. Scoring is the same as for the Block Game.

Fives-and-Threes

This game is also for two, three or four players (in partnership). Each player draws seven tiles, as for the Block Game. Lowest double takes first drop (starts). Every time the combined total of both ends of the leg is a multiple of three or five, the player completing the total, scores according to the following table:

Total at *both* ends	Score
3	1
5	1
6	2
9	3
10	2
12	4
15	8
18	6
20	4

Each 3 or 5 in the total scores one point; hence 15 is the top-scoring total (five 3's plus three 5's). When a player is blocked he

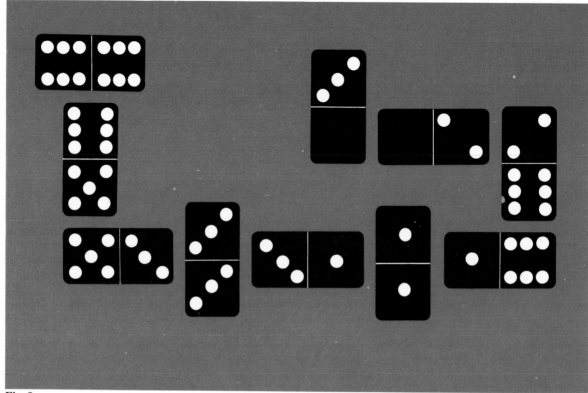

Fig. 3

must pass. The player (or partnership) who goes out scores an additional point.

Figure 3 shows a two-player game of Fives-and-Threes in progress. The plays, with points scored, were as follows:

Player A–double 1 (no score)
       B–1–6 (no score)
       A–1–3 (3 points)
       B–6–2 (1 point)
       A–2–blank (1 point)
       B–double 3 (2 points)
       A–3–5 (1 point)
       B–5–6 (2 points)
       A–blank–3 (3 points)
       B–double 6 (8 points)

Thus with ten tiles down, B leads by 13 points to 8.

The Star

The Star, or Cross, also known under several other names, is best as a four-player, non-partnership game.

Each player draws seven tiles and whoever holds the double-6 places it in the centre of the table. The next player must play a 6-spot but may place it *either* at right-angles to the starter *or* in line with it. The next three plays must add 6-spots to the starter so that a cross is formed. Once the cross has been formed players continue and score as in the Block Game. Any player holding the two remaining 6-spots has an advantage as he can secure one arm of the cross for at least one round.

Bergen

A good game for two, three or four players. In the two- and three-player versions, each draws six dominoes; four players draw five.

Lowest double is played and holder scores 2 points. If all doubles are in the boneyard, lowest tile is played but the owner does not score for it. Play rotates as usual except that if a player cannot match, he draws one tile which he must play if he is able. If he still cannot play, he passes.

The object of the game is to match both ends of the leg. When this is done, the player scores two points for a 'double-header'. If the domino at one end is a double, then the player matching it, or playing the double, gets 3 points for a 'triple-header'. (Hence the 2-point score for the double starter.)

The first player to get rid of all his tiles scores an additional point.

It pays to hold back doubles in this game in order to cap a double-header with a triple-header. As in most domino games, one cannot opt to pass.

There are a whole fund of other domino games, many drawn from oral tradition and with regional differences that are a social study in themselves. There are a few solitaire games. A very simple one calls for the player to draw five tiles from the pack. Starting with any domino, he plays from his hand as long as he can. When he is blocked, he again makes his hand up to five by drawing from the boneyard. He wins if he succeeds in playing out the whole pack.

Hints on Play

1) In most games it pays to go out first, so this is a primary aim.
2) With choice of plays, select from the longest suit. This enhances the chance of being able to add to the leg in the next round, particularly in a two-player game. As an extreme case, if every 5-spot were held, three tiles could be put down in succession without interference (a 5-spot at the end of the leg followed by the double-5 and another 5-spot). Naturally, if both legs can be controlled in this way there is considerable advantage.
3) Always conceal whether a play is made from choice or necessity.
4) With a little practice it is often possible to form some idea of opponents' hands. In a two-player game, if one player passes the second player may be able to identify certain tiles in the boneyard.
5) Mental arithmetic and a quick sight of exposed tiles are particularly useful in the harder games (e.g., Fives-and-Threes).

Card Games

Bridge, Poker, Bezique, Pinocle,
Piquet, Gin Rummy, Patience Games–
George Hervey

Bridge

Bridge is a game for four players only, two playing in partnership against two in partnership. It is played with the full pack of 52 cards, that rank in the order from Ace (high) to 2 (low). The suits rank in the order Spades (top), Hearts, Diamonds, Clubs (bottom). Spades and Hearts are known as the major suits, Diamonds and Clubs as the minor suits.

Partners are decided by every player drawing a card from a pack spread out on the table. The two who draw the two highest cards play as partners against the other two.

The player who draws the highest card has choice of seat. His partner sits facing him. The other two players occupy the remaining seats. This player also deals first. Thereafter the deal passes clockwise round the table.

The pack is shuffled by the player on the left of the dealer. The player on the right of the dealer cuts it, and the dealer completes the cut.

The dealer deals thirteen cards to each player, face downwards, one at a time, beginning with the player on his left. When the deal has been completed, the dealer makes the first call or bid. Thereafter the bidding passes clockwise round the table.

The Bidding

The purpose of calling is to establish which suit should be made the trump suit, or whether the hand shall be played without a trump suit; and here it is to be noted that a call of No-Trumps takes precedence over one of a suit.

When a player makes a bid he states the number of tricks in excess of six that he undertakes to win and in the denomination that he wishes to play. As an example, a bid of One Spade is an agreement to win seven tricks with Spades as the trump suit; in the same way a bid of Two No-Trumps is an agreement to win eight tricks without a trump suit. A bid of Six (small slam) is an agreement to win twelve tricks, and a bid of Seven (grand slam) an agreement to win all thirteen tricks.

Every bid must either name a greater number of tricks than the previous one, or an equal number of tricks in a higher denomination. If a player has no wish to contract to win tricks he may pass, which he does by saying 'No Bid'; and if all four players pass the hand is abandoned and the deal passes.

In his turn, any player may double a contract made by an opponent, and a player of the side that has been doubled may, in his turn, redouble. Doubling has the effect of increasing the score, whether the contract succeeds or fails, and redoubling increases the score still further. The size of the contract, however, is not increased.

The final contract is established when the last and highest bid has been followed by three passes. The player who was the first on his side to mention the denomination in the final contract becomes the declarer. The opponent on his left makes the opening lead (thereafter the player who wins a trick leads to the next) and the partner of the declarer exposes his cards on the table. The declarer plays his partner's cards as well as his own, and the partner (dummy) takes no part in the game other than to draw attention to any irregularity and ask his partner if he has no card of a suit in which he has renounced.

In illustrative examples it is customary to denote the four players by the cardinal points of the compass. The example of a bidding sequence that follows illustrates some of the points mentioned in this article.

South (dealer)	West	North	East
1 ♦	No Bid	1 ♥	1 ♠
1 No-Trump	2 ♠	3 ♦	No Bid
3 No-Trumps	Double	No Bid	No Bid
4 ♦	No Bid	5 ♦	Double
Redouble	No Bid	No Bid	No Bid

The contract, therefore, is Five Diamonds redoubled. West will make the opening lead. North will expose his cards on the table as dummy, and South will play North's cards as well as his own.

The players play their cards in clockwise rotation. If he is able to, a player must follow suit to the card led; if he is unable to he may either discard or play a trump. A trick is won by the player who plays the highest card of the led-suit, or the highest trump.

After a deal has been played, the players record the score on a marker, or sheet of paper, ruled as in the accompanying diagram. All scores are entered either above or below the bold horizontal line. Scores made by one's own side are recorded in the left-hand column; scores made by the opponents in the right-hand column.

Scoring below the Line
The only scores entered below the horizontal line are those made

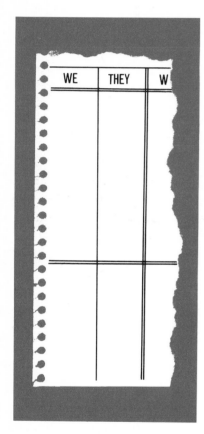

WE	THEY	W

by a side which has bid and made its contract. The trick values for the various contracts are:

No-Trumps: first trick 40 points, each subsequent trick 30 points.
Spades and Hearts: each trick 30 points.
Diamonds and Clubs: each trick 20 points.

The trick score is multiplied by two if doubled, and by four if redoubled.

When a side has scored 100 points below the line, either in one contract or in two or more, it has made a game. A line is drawn across the score sheet cancelling any part-score that the opponents may have made. A new game begins with both sides at love score.

A side that has won a game becomes vulnerable. If it fails to make a contract it is subject to higher penalties, but it scores increased bonuses if it does. Vulnerability does not affect the points for scoring the tricks contracted for.

Scoring above the Line
All other scores by either side are recorded above the horizontal line.

If a side makes tricks in excess of its contract, it scores:
If undoubled: trick value for each trick.
If doubled: not vulnerable 100 points for each trick, vulnerable 200 points for each trick.
If redoubled: not vulnerable 200 points for each trick, vulnerable 400 points for each trick.

If a side fails to make its contract it loses:
If undoubled: not vulnerable 50 points for each trick, vulnerable 100 points for each trick.
If doubled: not vulnerable 100 points for the first trick and 200 for each subsequent trick, vulnerable 200 points and 300 points respectively.
If redoubled: not vulnerable 200 points for the first trick and 400 points for each subsequent trick, vulnerable 400 points and 600 points respectively.

If a side is doubled or redoubled and makes its contract it scores a bonus of 50 points.
If a side bids and makes a grand slam it scores 1000 points not

vulnerable and 1500 vulnerable.

If a side bids and makes a small slam it scores 500 points not vulnerable and 750 vulnerable.

If a player holds in his hand all four Aces and the contract is in No-Trumps, he scores 150 points.

If a player holds in his hand all five honours (**A K Q J 10**) of the trump suit, he scores 150 points, and if he holds any four of them 100 points.

The side that is first to win two games wins the rubber, on the result of which the stakes are settled. If a side wins the rubber in two games it scores a bonus of 700 points, if it wins it in two games to one it scores a bonus of 500 points.

If a game is brought to an end before a rubber is completed, a side that is a game ahead scores a bonus of 300 points, and a side with a part score in an unfinished game scores a bonus of 50 points.

Bridge is a partnership game, as whist was before it. It is not a difficult game, but it is a complicated one, because for long it has been recognized that in a partnership game the most successful player is he who is best able to combine his cards with those held by his partner. As a result, bridge players have developed a large number of systems and conventional bids, designed to enable the partners to give each other as much information as possible about their hands.

For tournament play and for play in clubs where the stakes are high it is important for players to understand these systems and conventions. For social play and for play in clubs where the stakes are low, and the game of more importance than the money that is to be won, they are comparatively unimportant, and most players get along quite well with a simple system, the Two Clubs System, popularly called Utility, and that might be named Basic Bridge.

Players no longer value a hand by honour tricks but by means of a point count. An Ace is counted as 4 points, a King as 3, a Queen as 2 and a Jack as 1. Altogether, therefore, there are 40 points in the pack, and an average hand contains 10 points. Some players add points if they hold a void or singleton of a suit, but it only adds to the complications of the game.

It must be appreciated, however, that the strength of a hand lies not only in the high cards that it contains, but also in the distribution of the suits. A hand that contains 13 points must be opened, but the longer a suit is the less the number of points necessary for a bid.

With a reasonably good 5-card suit the point count may be reduced to 11 or 12, and with a 6-card suit, or with two 5-card suits, the count may be no more than 10, sometimes even less.

The criterion is that the hand should contain at least two defensive tricks (Ace, or King-Queen) because the opponents may have enough to outbid your side and play the hand; four playing tricks (that is enough to win about four tricks without any help from partner) and, above all, a satisfactory rebid, because when a player opens the bidding (and his partner has not passed) he promises to make a further bid if partner responds with One in a higher-ranking suit or with Two in a lower-ranking suit.

The hands below qualify for an opening bid of One Spade:

(a)

(b)

(c)

Hand (a) has a good Spade suit and is strongly distributional; hand (b) can safely be rebid at the level of Two; and in hand (c) Spades may first be bid because the Hearts can be bid if partner responds with a bid of Two in either minor suit.

An opening bid of Two of a suit (other than of Clubs) is forcing for one round. It is made with a hand that is so strong that the player must make certain that he will have a chance to bid again. With hands such as:

it is best to open with Two Spades. If only One Spade is bid there is the risk that everyone, including partner, may pass and a game be lost. With either of these hands it would be unwise to make an opening game bid, because it gives no escape from defeat if partner holds the wrong cards.

Over an opening bid of Two Spades, Two Hearts or Two Diamonds, if partner holds a biddable suit he will bid it at the lowest level; if he holds no biddable suit but a count of 10 to 12 points he will bid Three No-Trumps; if he holds no biddable suit and lacks the count to bid Three No-Trumps he will support his partner's suit with **x x x** or **Q x** of the suit and a count of at least 5 points. He must not pass and if his hand fails to measure up to any of these requirements he will bid Two No-Trumps (called a negative response).

An opening bid of Two Clubs is a conventional bid that may be made even if the player holds no card of the suit. The bid is forcing

(a)

(b)

to game and is made either with a hand of balanced pattern and 24 or more points; or with a hand of unbalanced pattern but with a reasonable prospect of making nine tricks even if partner holds nothing. Either of the hands opposite qualify for an opening bid of Two Clubs.

Hand (a) is too strong for a No-Trump bid, and hand (b) is better opened with Two Clubs, which is forcing to game, than Two Spades, which is forcing for only one round.

Over an opening bid of Two Clubs, partner, if he holds a weak hand, must make the negative response of Two Diamonds. If, however, he holds a reasonably good suit and a top honour outside he will bid the suit; with 8 or 9 points including two Aces he will bid Two No-Trumps, and with the equivalent of three Kings and a Jack he will bid Three No-Trumps.

Opening bids of Three or Four of a suit are pre-emptive. The player bids as high as he can afford with the aim of preventing the opponents from entering the auction, or forcing one of them to take the risk of bidding at a level that is dangerously high. Postulating that the hand is likely to be doubled and defeated, the player who pre-empts rides for a fall of 500 points, because this loss is cheaper than if the opponents are able to score game. From this it follows that a pre-emptive bid is made in the expectation of going not more than three down if not vulnerable and two down if vulnerable.

No-Trump bidding is probably simpler than suit bidding, because it is largely a matter of counting points. With 40 points in the pack, if a side holds 37 points normally it has enough for a grand slam, if 33 points enough for a small slam, and if 25 points enough for game.

An opening bid of One No-Trump is made with a count of 16 to 18 points, and a balanced distribution (4-3-3-3, 4-4-3-2, or 5-3-3-2) but the 5-card suit, if one is held, should be a minor.

As 25 points are enough for game, partner will bid Three No-Trumps if he holds 9 points, and Two No-Trumps if he holds 7 or 8 points, leaving it to opener to pass with a minimum or bid game with a maximum.

An opening bid of Two No-Trumps is made with a balanced hand and a count of 20 to 22 points; partner will raise to Three No-Trumps if he holds a minimum of 5 points.

An opening bid of Three No-Trumps is tactical. It shows a hand that contains a solid minor (never major) suit and altogether

one that has a reasonable chance of winning nine tricks if partner
has one or two top cards in the right places. This hand:

qualifies for an opening bid of Three No-Trumps. With seven
tricks in the black suits partner needs only a few points in the red
ones to guarantee nine tricks being made. Normally he will pass
the bid, but if he doubts that the contract will be made, or if an
opponent doubles, he will know from his own cards that there is
an escape to Four Clubs.

A simple response to One No-Trump in a suit, other than Clubs,
is a weak bid that promises no more than a 5-card or 6-card suit
and 7 points at most. The opener should pass because partner has
suggested that there is no chance of game and that the hand will

(a)

(b)

(c)

(d)

probably play better in his suit than in No-Trumps.

With 9 or more points, and a 5-card or longer suit, partner will respond with a forcing bid of Three in his suit.

With hands (a) and (b) Two Spades should be bid because there is reason to think that One No-Trump is unlikely to be made. With hand (c) Three Spades should be bid and partner will either bid Four Spades or correct to Three No-Trumps. Hand (d) is a maximum and offers good prospects of a slam. Three Spades should be bid.

A bid of Two Clubs, in response to partner's One No-Trump, is known as the Stayman Convention. It is an artificial bid that asks partner to bid his better 4-card major suit, or Two Diamonds if he has not got one.

West   **East**

Bidding
1 No-Trump	2♣
2♥	4♥
No Bid	

The best contract has been found. Game in Hearts is reasonably certain. Without the convention, East would have no alternative except to raise West's bid of One No-Trump to Three. The combined count of 27 points is more than adequate, but the contract might fail if a Club is led.

If the opening bid is Two No-Trumps, a bid of Three Clubs by the responder performs the same function.

In both cases, however, it must be remembered that the player who launches the convention must have a safe landing place.

Apart from the opening bid of Two Clubs, a number of other bids are forcing to game.

The most important, because it is the most frequent, is a jump bid in a new suit. It is, however, much the same if the opener makes a jump re-bid in a new suit after his partner has responded.

South	West	North	East
1♥	No Bid	1♠	No Bid
3♣	No Bid		

North must not pass. South's bid of Three Clubs establishes a game-forcing situation.

Then, too, a number of sequences create forcing situations by reason of their logic.

South	West	North	East
1♠	No Bid	2♠	No Bid
3♣	No Bid		

Since North has made a very weak response, the fact that South has made a further bid, when there was no need for him to do so, shows that he holds a strong hand. North must not pass.

South	West	North	East
1♠	No Bid	2♦	No Bid
2 No-Trumps	No Bid	3♠	No Bid

South must not pass because North is clearly inviting him to choose between playing the hand in Three No-Trumps or Four Spades.

When the bidding of the partners has shown that between them they hold a very powerful combination of hands they must give consideration to bidding a slam.

Under normal conditions, prospects of a slam are good when a player holds enough to make a positive response to a forcing bid; when the combined hands contain a count of at least 33 points; when a player holds enough for an opening bid and his partner has already opened with a bid of Two; when a player has enough to make an opening bid and his partner has opened the bidding and made a jump rebid.

Before a slam may be bid with confidence the partners must know whether or not they control the suits, because without Aces or voids in a suit, the opponents may be in a position to defeat the slam before the declarer can take the lead.

The Blackwood Convention is the simplest way to find out if control of a suit is held. When the trump suit has been agreed on, either by direct support or by implication, or if a forcing situation has been established, a bid of Four No-Trumps by either partner demands that the other partner shall show how many Aces he holds. This the player does by bidding Five Clubs if he holds no Ace or all four, Five Diamonds if he holds one Ace, Five Hearts if he holds two, and Five Spades if he holds three. Then, if the player who has bid Four No-Trumps continues by bidding Five No-Trumps over partner's response, he asks his partner to show how many Kings he holds. Partner bids Six Clubs if he lacks a King, Six Diamonds if he holds one King, Six Hearts if he holds two, Six Spades if he holds three, and Six No-Trumps if he holds all four.

West   **East**

Bidding

1 ♥	2 ♠
3 ♦	4 No-Trumps
5 ♥	5 No-Trumps
6 ♥	7 ♠
No Bid	

The convention is one that must be used with discretion, because it contains a number of pitfalls for the unwary. It enables a player to find out how many Aces and Kings his partner holds, but not which ones, and those he holds may be in the wrong places. Then, too, if partner's response shows that he lacks the necessary number of Aces, the partnership may find that it has been carried out of its depth. Particular care is needed if the final contract is to be in a minor suit.

When a player has opened the auction, the partners on the opposite side are known as the defenders, and the defender on the left of the opening bidder must bear in mind that if he plans to make a bid he is at a disadvantage, because he knows nothing about his partner's hand. By contrary, the partner of the opening bidder may hold a fairly strong hand, and he has the advantage of knowing that he can rely on one facing him.

To make an overcall as a defender, therefore, points are less of a guide than how many tricks one is likely to win if left to play the hand, and overcalling should be governed by the Rule of Two and Three and the Principle of Risk versus Gain. The Rule of Two and Three means that the bidder should have a reasonable expectation of winning within two tricks of his contract if he is vulnerable and

three tricks if he is not vulnerable; the Principle of Risk versus Gain means that any bid that he makes should stand to gain more than it may lose. If South has opened the auction with One Diamond, West, by the Rule of Two and Three, has enough, even if vulnerable, to bid One Heart if he holds the hand on the opposite page because he may fairly expect to win five tricks (three in Hearts and one each in Diamonds and Clubs). And if West's hand is:

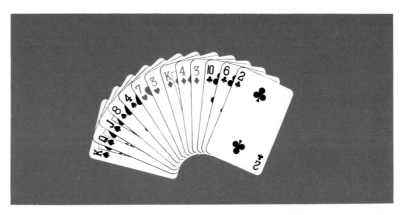

the Principle of Risk versus Gain permits him to shade the requirements of the Rule of Two and Three and bid One Spade if he is not vulnerable. The bid may, of course, result in his winning only three tricks for a loss of 700 points, but against this he has prevented North from bidding Hearts at the level of One (and he may not be good enough to bid at the level of Two) and if North obtains the final declaration, West has shown his partner the best suit to lead. Nor must it be forgotten that if West plays in Spades and wins only three tricks, the opponents have almost certainly missed a slam.

A jump overcall shows strength but is not forcing. The only game-forcing bid is one made in the suit bid by an opponent.

On the whole, however, when a player has bid One of a suit, it is usually better for a defender to make a take-out double rather than a weak overbid. The double requests partner to bid his best suit, and normally he will do so, but if the suit has been bid by the opponents he may either bid No-Trumps or, with length in the suit, pass—thereby announcing that he prefers to play for a penalty. The weaker his hand, the more important it is that he bids, and with 9 or more points he should make a jump bid to show that his hand is better than a minimum.

When an opening bid has been followed by two passes the fourth hand must do his best to find a bid. It is cowardly to pass because the opposing contract is not enough to give game, and a bid by fourth hand (known as a protective bid) should be made on limited strength. A take-out double is based on about 12 points, even less if the distribution is favourable, and a bid of One No-Trump may be made with a count of from 11 to 14 points and not necessarily with a guard in the opponent's suit. A suit may be bid with quite a weak hand.

South deals and bids One Heart. West and North pass. East holds:

(a)

(b)

(c)

(d)

With hand (a) East should double; with hand (b) he should bid One No-Trump; with hand (c) One Spade; and with hand (d) Two Clubs.

In making these bids East takes into consideration that his partner is in a difficult position to bid, because he does not know how strong the hand over him is; and as the partner of the opening bidder has passed he cannot be holding more than 4 or 5 points.

The Play

The player on the left of the final declarer has to make the opening lead. It must be chosen with care because the choice of a good or a bad lead may decide whether or not the contract is made.

Against a No-Trump contract, if partner has bid, it is usually best to lead his suit, unless the player on lead holds a singleton of the suit or has a good suit of his own. With two cards of partner's suit the higher should be led; with three cards the highest, unless the suit is headed by the Ace, King or Queen, when the lowest should be preferred. With two honours in partner's suit the higher should be led; and with a sequence (three or more cards of adjacent rank) the highest should be led. In all other cases the fourth highest should be led.

When a player leads his own suit he should lead the fourth highest of it, unless it contains a sequence (when he should lead the highest). It the suit is a long one, headed by the Ace and King with an entry in another suit, the King should be led, and with an intermediate honour sequence e.g., **A Q J x** or **K J 10 x**, the higher of the two touching honours should be led.

Against a suit contract, if partner has bid a suit, it is usually best to lead it. If he has not, and the player on lead has to lead from his own suit, he should give preference to leading the top card of an honour sequence. He should avoid leading a card that might enable the declarer to win a trick with a card that might be captured e.g., leading the Ace from **A Q x**. The lead of a trump card is a good lead if the bidding has suggested that the dummy will be able to trump side suits.

If the bidding at bridge is, to some extent, subject to clear and precise explanation, the play of the cards is not. The number of deals reaches the astronomical total of 54,000 quadrillion; inevitably, therefore, signals between partners, when to win a trick, when not to, and the like, are all the time subject to modification by reason of the bidding, the cards that have been played, the cards that are to be seen in dummy, and those that are known to be held by the other players. The play of the cards, in fact, is essentially a matter of practice, of learning from past experience what to do and what not to do when a similar situation occurs. In the restricted compass of an article little can be done except to present a number of explanatory deals that are not beyond the capacity of most players, but which are frequently mishandled at the card table because a player fails to think along the right lines.

Declarer's Play
A finesse is rarely a good way to try for an extra trick, because it succeeds or fails on the position of one card—giving the declarer a mere fifty-fifty chance.

West   East

Love all. West dealt.

West	North	East	South
1 No-Trump	No Bid	3 No-Trumps	No Bid
No Bid	No Bid		

North led the ♦ **4**, West played ♦ **5** from dummy and South ♦ **J**. West won with ♦ **A**. West had eight tricks (two Spades, one Heart, one Diamond and four Clubs) on top, and had no need to risk finessing dummy's ♠ **J** for the ninth trick. As South had played the ♦ **J** at the first trick, it was a reasonable assumption that North held ♦ **10**, so, at the second trick, West led ♦ **3** and after North had played ♦ **7**, West played ♦ **9** from dummy. It drew ♦ **K** from South and left dummy's ♦ **Q** good for the ninth trick.

West   East

Game all. South dealt.

South	West	North	East
1 ♥	2 ♦	4 ♥	5 ♦
No Bid	No Bid	No Bid	

North led the ♥ **Q** and West won with ♥ **A**. West led the ♦ **Q** and North played the ♦ **8**. West overtook with ♦ **A**, won three tricks in Spades, ruffed the ♥ **6** on the table, and got off lead to South with a Diamond. South had no Diamond to lead; if he led either a Spade or a Heart, West would discard a Club from hand and ruff in dummy; if he led a Club he would set up dummy's King.

West's play derived from the fact that as South, vulnerable, had opened the auction he had to be holding the ♦ K and the ♣ A Q otherwise he hardly had his bid. If, at the second trick, West had run the ♦ Q (instead of winning with dummy's ♦ A) South would have won with the ♦ K, got off lead with the ♦ 7, and waited for the two tricks in Clubs to fall into his lap.

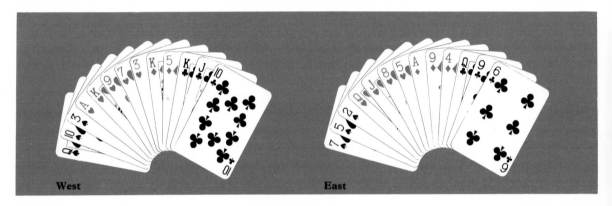

West   East

North-South game, East-West love. South dealt.

South	West	North	East
1 ♠	2 ♥	No Bid	4 ♥
No Bid	No Bid	No Bid	

North led the ♠ 4, South won with ♠ A and returned the ♠ 6. West played the ♠ 10, and as North had led from K 8 4 the contract was safe because North and South could never win more than two tricks in Spades and the ♣ A.

If at the second trick West had played ♠ Q, North would have won with the ♠ K and returned the ♠ 8 for South to win with the ♠ J and defeat the contract with the ♣ A.

Correct thinking had enabled West to find the right way home. North's lead of the ♠ 4 could not be the higher of a doubleton, nor the highest of a tripleton, because West himself held the ♠ 3 and he could see the ♠ 2 in dummy. It could not be fourth highest, because it would leave room for only three Spades in South's hand, and this is out of the question in fact of his opening bid of One Spade. West's ♠ 4, therefore, was either a singleton or the lowest of a tripleton. If it was a singleton, South's Spades would be **A K J 9 8 6**, and, even if he had not won the first trick with ♠ **K** (instead of with ♠ **A**) he would certainly have continued with a top card and not with the ♠ **6**. As a result, West was able to deduce that North's lead was either from **K x 4**, **J x 4**, or **x x 4**, and it had to be from **K x 4** as with either of the other two combinations the highest card would have been led.

West   East

Game all. North dealt.

North	East	South	West
No Bid	No Bid	No Bid	2 ♣
No Bid	2 ♦	No Bid	2 No-Trumps
No Bid	3 ♦	No Bid	3 No-Trumps
No Bid	No Bid	No Bid	

North led the ♣ **Q**. West won with ♣ **A** and led ♦ **J** to ♦ **Q** in dummy. South (who held **K x x** of Diamonds) could not afford to win with ♦ **K** and played low. West continued by leading dummy's ♦ **10** and, once again, South could not afford to part with ♦ **K**. So West played the ♦ **5** from his hand, abandoned the suit and led a Spade from the table, playing ♠ **Q** from his hand after South had played ♠ **3**. When the finesse held, West was able to claim his contract with two tricks in Spades, two in Hearts, three in Diamonds and two in Clubs.

It is tempting for West to win the ♦ **A** at the second trick (in case the ♦ **K** is a singleton) and continue with ♦ **J** if ♦ **K** has not come down under ♦ **A.** It wins the contract if either opponent started with ♦ **K x** or if the suit breaks **x x** and **K x x** (as it did) and the King is used to capture the Jack. A good player, however, would hold up ♦ **K.** Dummy is killed and West is held to eight tricks at best.

West   East

Love all. West dealt.

West	North	East	South
1♦	No Bid	2♣	No Bid
2 No-Trumps	No Bid	3 No-Trumps	No Bid
No Bid	No Bid		

North led ♥ **7** and dummy's ♥ **Q** held the trick. West could not make his contract without bringing in dummy's Clubs, and he had to prevent South from taking the lead because if South came on lead he would lead a Heart through West's King and the contract would certainly be defeated.

West made the correct play of leading dummy's ♣ **3** and playing ♣ **9** from his own hand after South had played low. If North held the ♣ **J** he would be welcome to win the trick with it because he is harmless on lead and West can win nine tricks (two Spades, one Heart, one Diamond and five Clubs) no matter how North continues. If South held the ♣ **J**, West's ♣ **9** would have won the trick and now he has ten tricks on top.

Playing off the Ace, King and Queen of Clubs loses the contract if North has a singleton of the suit and South four to the Jack; even a successful finesse of the ♦ **Q** brings in only eight tricks.

When a player is able to learn, from the bidding and play, the position of the unseen cards, he is said to count the hand. It is an important feature of declarer's play.

West   East

Game all. West dealt.

West	North	East	South
1 ♥	2 ♣	2 ♥	No Bid
4 ♥	No Bid	No Bid	No Bid

North won ♣ A and ♣ K (on which South played ♣ 7 and ♣ 4) and continued with ♣ J. South ruffed with ♥ 10 and West over-ruffed with ♥ Q. West led ♥ K. North played ♥ 5 and South discarded a Spade. West continued with ♥ 3. North won with ♥ A and got off lead with ♥ 6. After winning this trick, West won three tricks in Diamonds and both opponents followed suit all three times.

West now had a count of the hand. As North was known to have started with three Hearts and six Clubs, and he had followed three times to Diamonds, there was room in his hand for not more than one Spade. To make certain of the contract, therefore, West led ♠ 5 and after North had played ♠ 8, he won in dummy with ♠ A, and finessed with confidence against South for the Queen.

Defenders' Play
The play of the defenders is always more difficult than the play of the declarer, because each partner has to combine his hand with

an unseen one, and not with an exposed dummy. Their position is made easier by means of a number of recognized signals and communication plays, but, on the whole, they are always at a slight disadvantage.

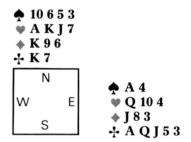

♠ 10 6 5 3
♥ A K J 7
♦ K 9 6
♣ K 7

♠ A 4
♥ Q 10 4
♦ J 8 3
♣ A Q J 5 3

Love all. East dealt.

East	South	West	North
1 ♣	1 ♠	No Bid	3 ♠
No Bid	4 ♠	No Bid	No Bid
No Bid			

West led ♣ 8. East won ♣ A and ♣ J, and then led ♣ Q because South had played the ♣ 4 and ♣ 9, and West's opening lead of the ♣ 8, therefore, marked South with the ♣ 10, and there was nothing to lose by giving dummy a ruff.

After South had won the third trick by ruffing East's ♣ Q with dummy's ♠ 3, he led ♠ 10 from the table, and allowed it to run when East played ♠ 4. South now abandoned Spades; won ♦ A, entered dummy with ♦ K, ruffed dummy's last Diamond in the closed hand, and put East on lead with a Spade. The contract was now made, because East had to lead either a Heart into dummy's tenace, or a Club, which would give South a ruff and discard.

When the declarer and his dummy hold a preponderance of trumps, and when the dummy hand holds an honour combination which cannot be led to or from without the loss of a trick, the defenders should be alert to the fact that the declarer is very likely to play for a throw-in. East had nothing to gain by holding up ♠ A; winning it at the fourth trick and getting off lead by leading ♠ 4 could not have harmed the defence, because South's bidding does not make sense if he holds less than five Spades to the King, Queen and Jack, and ♦ **A**.

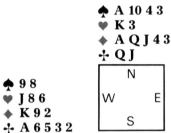

♠ **A 10 4 3**
♥ **K 3**
♦ **A Q J 4 3**
♣ **Q J**

♠ **9 8**
♥ **J 8 6**
♦ **K 9 2**
♣ **A 6 5 3 2**

Game all. North dealt.

North	East	South	West
1♦	1♥	1♠	No Bid
4♠	No Bid	No Bid	No Bid

West led ♥ **J** on which South played dummy's ♥ **3**, East ♥ **9** and South ♥ **2**. Despite East's play of an encouragement card, West rejected the Heart continuation and won ♣ **A**. After East had played ♣ **8**, West continued the suit, for East to win with ♣ **K** and break the contract with ♥ **A**.

West's play of ♣ **A** at the second trick was well considered. It was clear to him that the ♦ **K** was a dead duck, and, from the bidding, that South had almost certainly the required ten tricks in Spades and Diamonds. The only hope of breaking the contract, therefore, was to find East with ♣ **K**. To have continued with a Heart would have put the lead in East's hand. He might have led a Club, but he might not, and West's play was made to leave nothing to chance. There was no hurry for East to win ♥ **A**: it would not run away.

♠ **A 7 4 3**
♥ **J**
♦ **K 10 9 8 7 3**
♣ **9 2**

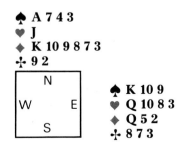

♠ **K 10 9**
♥ **Q 10 8 3**
♦ **Q 5 2**
♣ **8 7 3**

North-South game, East-West love. North dealt.

North	East	South	West
No Bid	No Bid	1 No-Trump	No Bid
2 ♣ (Stayman)	No Bid	2 ♥	No Bid
3 No-Trumps	No Bid	No Bid	No Bid

West led ♣ Q. South won with ♣ A and led ♦ J on which West played the ♦ 4 and South ♦ 3 from dummy. East made the good play of winning with ♦ Q and leading ♠ K, in order to knock out dummy's ♠ A.

If South had held ♦ A he would have won it before leading ♦ J, and ♦ J could hardly be a singleton in face of South's opening bid of One No-Trump. It was, therefore, reasonable for East to assume that South had started with ♦ J 6 and West with ♦ A 4. South could make his contract only by bringing in dummy's Diamonds, and to do this he needed ♠ A on the table as an entry to the suit after West's ♦ A had been taken from him. East saw what was coming, and countered it by removing dummy's ♠ A before South was able to remove West's ♦ A.

In order to get rid of dummy's ♠ A, it was vital for East to lead the ♠ K at the third trick. If he had led either ♠ 10 or ♠ 9, South would have been able to protect ♠ A in his dummy by winning the trick with ♠ Q in his own hand.

♠ A K Q 10
♥ J 10
♦ 9 4
♣ K 10 9 8 4

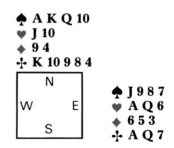

♠ J 9 8 7
♥ A Q 6
♦ 6 5 3
♣ A Q 7

North-South love, East-West game. West dealt.

West	North	East	South
No Bid	1 ♣	No Bid	1 ♥
No Bid	1 ♠	No Bid	2 No-Trumps
No Bid	3 No-Trumps	No Bid	No Bid
No Bid			

West led ♦ **Q** and South played ♦ **7**. West continued with ♦ **J**, South won with ♦ **K**, and led ♣ **J** on which West played ♣ **3** and South ♣ **4** from dummy.

It was clear from the bidding and play of the first two tricks that South's honour strength consisted of ♥ **K**, ♦ **A K** and ♣ **J**.

In theory, therefore, South could make his contract with three tricks in Spades, one in Hearts, two in Diamonds and three in Clubs. In order to defeat it, East found the fine defence of winning the third trick with ♣ **Q**, cashing ♥ **A** and continuing with the ♥ **6**.

If South played low from his hand and won with dummy's ♥ **J** he would be held to eight tricks, because he could never reach his hand to win ♦ **A**. A Club from dummy would be won by East with the Ace, ♣ **7** from East would lock South on the table, and East would eventually come to the setting trick with ♠ **J**.

On the other hand, if South won the fifth trick with ♥ **K**, and then cashed ♦ **A**, he could never prevent East from defeating the contract by winning the ♣ **A** and ♥ **Q**.

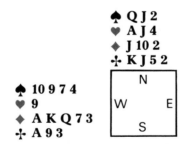

♠ Q J 2
♥ A J 4
♦ J 10 2
♣ K J 5 2

♠ 10 9 7 4
♥ 9
♦ A K Q 7 3
♣ A 9 3

Love all. South dealt.

South	West	North	East
1♠	2♦	2♠	No Bid
2♥	No Bid	4♠	No Bid
No Bid	No Bid		

West won ♦ **A** and ♦ **K** on which East played ♦ **5** and ♦ **6**, and South ♦ **4** and ♦ **8**. West continued with ♦ **Q** on which East played ♦ **9** and South won with ♠ **5**. South now led ♣ **7**. West found the killing defence.

South was holding exactly five Spades. He could not be holding less because his bid of Three Hearts showed a willingness to play in

Spades at the level of Three. He must be holding four Hearts to the King and Queen to have justified bidding the suit on the second round of the auction, so he could not be holding more than five Spades, because then he would have ten cold tricks in the major suits, enough to run to his contract and with no need to play a Club at the fourth trick.

It was clear to West, therefore, that South had nine tricks (five Spades and four Hearts) by straight leads, and that he was trying to grab his tenth trick with dummy's ♣ K, on the assumption that ♣ A was held by West (on account of his bid) and that he would not win it, but play low on the chance that South might play ♣ J from dummy and East might be holding ♣ Q.

It might have been this way, but West found a much surer way to defeat the contract. As South had ruffed the third round of Diamonds with ♠ 5, ♠ 3 was almost certainly with East. So West won the fifth trick with ♣ A and led ♦ 7. This way, if South ruffed with dummy's ♠ 2, East would over-ruff with ♠ 3 and force South to win with ♠ 6. It would set up West's ♠ 10 as a winner because he would be holding four trumps and neither South nor his dummy would hold more than three. Nor would it help South to ruff ♦ 7 with dummy's ♠ J. With dummy's trumps reduced to the Q 2 West would always come to a trick with the 10, to put the contract one down.

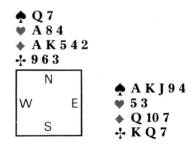

```
              ♠ Q 7
              ♥ A 8 4
              ♦ A K 5 4 2
              ♣ 9 6 3
         ┌─────────────┐
         │      N      │        ♠ A K J 9 4
         │             │        ♥ 5 3
         │ W         E │        ♦ Q 10 7
         │             │        ♣ K Q 7
         │      S      │
         └─────────────┘
```

North-South love, East-West game. North dealt.

North	East	South	West
1 ♦	1 ♠	2 ♥	No Bid
3 ♥	No Bid	4 ♥	No Bid
No Bid	No Bid		

West led ♠ 8, South played ♠ 7 from dummy, East won with

♠ J and South played ♠ 2. East continued by winning ♠ A, on which South played ♠ 6 and West ♠ 3.

It was tempting for East to lead ♣ K and so set up a trick in the suit, but the danger of this play was that South might be holding a doubleton Diamond. If he was, South would win the third trick with ♣ A (the bidding marked him as holding this card) win dummy's ♦ A and ♦ K and ruff a Diamond from the table in the closed hand. This way, two Diamonds would be set up in dummy and South could draw the outstanding trumps in three rounds, ending in dummy, and discard two losers from his hand on the established Diamonds.

At the third trick, East made the better, indeed the best, play of leading ♠ K. South had to ruff it in dummy (if he did not East would continue with ♠ 9) and was left with no way to bring in dummy's two established Diamonds after he had won the ♦ A and ♦ K on the table and ruffed the third round in his own hand.

Poker

Poker is a game of skill. By this is meant that, in the long run, the experienced player will win and the inexperienced lose. If we exclude the ubiquitous bridge, it is the national game of the U.S.A., played extensively in the mining and lumber camps, and much favoured by the professional gamblers of the Mississippi steamboats. It is, perhaps, for these reasons, as well as the fact that there is little more in the game than betting that one's hand of five cards will be the best at the table, that the game has been given a bad name and considered by some a pure gamble.

The game has many variations, far more than has any other card game, but a player who knows the values of the poker hands and the principles of betting, can play any variation without difficulty.

The standard game, commonly called straight poker, but more correctly straight draw poker, is played with the 52-card pack. The cards rank in the order from Ace (high) to 2 (low). The suits are of equal value.

In theory the game may be played by any reasonable number of players, but five, six or seven is considered the ideal.

To determine who deals first the traditional method is to deal the pack face upwards round the table until a Jack appears. The player to whom it is dealt is first dealer, and thereafter the deal, after every hand, passes clockwise round the table.

The dealer deals five cards face downwards, one at a time, to each player. The player's object is to obtain the best poker hand possible, and he has one opportunity to improve the hand dealt to him by discarding any number of his cards and refilling his hand from the undealt cards of the pack. Altogether there are nine classes of poker hands. These, with the odds against them being dealt to a player, are set out below, in descending order of value.

Straight flush. A sequence of five cards of the same suit, the Ace either high, e.g.,

or low, e.g.,

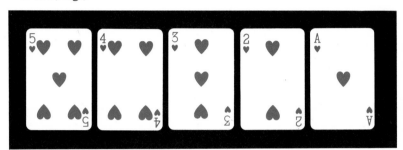

It takes its rank from the highest card. 64,973 to 1.

Four of a kind (commonly called Fours). Any four cards of the same rank and any unmatched card, e.g.,

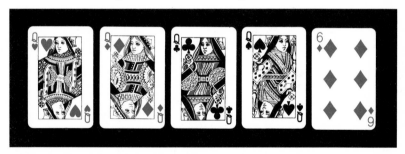

The odds against it are 4,164 to 1.

Full house. Any three cards of the same rank and two other cards of the same rank, e.g.,

It takes its rank from the threesome. 693 to 1.

Flush. Five cards all of the same suit, e.g.,

It takes its rank from the highest card and if equal from the second highest, and so on. 508 to 1.

Straight. Any five cards in sequence and not of the same suit. An Ace may be high, e.g.,

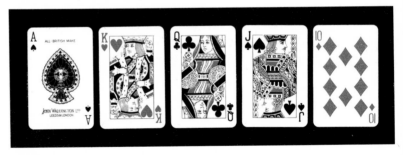

or low, e.g.,

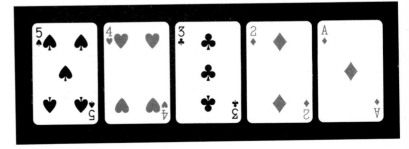

It takes its rank from the card at the higher end of the sequence of five. 254 to 1.

Three of a kind (commonly called Threes). Three cards of the same rank and two unmatched cards, e.g.,

The odds against it are 46 to 1.

Two pairs. Two cards of the same rank, two other cards of the same rank, and an unmatched card, e.g.,

It takes its rank from the higher pair, if equal from the lower, and if again equal from the unmatched card. 20 to 1.

One pair. Two cards of the same rank and three unmatched cards, e.g.,

If equal it takes its rank from the highest unmatched card if again equal from the second highest and if again equal from the lowest. 15 to 11.

Highest card. Any five unmatched cards, e.g.,

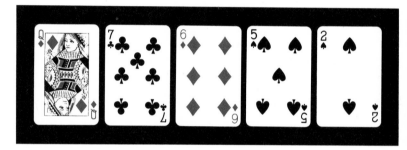

It takes its rank from the highest card, if equal from the second highest, and so on. Evens.

In the event, unlikely but not impossible, of two or more players holding exactly equal hands the stakes are divided.

There is no scoring. Throughout the game the players put their money (or its equivalent in chips) on the table in front of them. At the end of every hand, a player has either won more money (or chips) or lost his stake.

The Play
The game begins by the player on the left of the dealer putting up an agreed amount, known as the ante. For the sake of convenience of explanation we will assume that it is one chip. Now the player on his left puts up a straddle of two chips.

The cards are dealt, and, after looking at his hand, the player on the left of the straddle (known as first to speak) has the option of playing or not. If he decides not to play, he throws his cards face downwards on the table and takes no further interest in the deal in progress. If, however, he decides to play, he puts up four chips. Each of the other players, clockwise round the table, has the same decision to make: not to play, to come into the game for the same stake as the previous player, or to come in raising the stake until the agreed maximum is reached. Practice varies. In some circles doubling is allowed indefinitely: 4−8−16−32−64−etc.; in others a limit is placed on raising stakes and after 16 the stakes are increased by 8s i.e., to 24–32–40–etc.

When it comes round to the ante and straddle, they have the option of coming into the game by raising their stakes to the appropriate amount, or throwing in their hands and sacrificing what they have already put up.

If no player comes into the game, the straddle recovers his two chips and takes the one chip put up by the ante.

Staking usually takes a little time, because it is open to those players who have come into the game, and who have been doubled by a subsequent player, to increase their stakes. This progressive staking continues until no-one increases the stake, or the agreed limit has been reached.

The Exchange

When everyone has staked, those remaining in the game have a chance to try to improve their hands by exchanging cards for those in the undealt part of the pack. The dealer ignores those who have thrown in their hands, but, clockwise round the table, asks those left in the game if they want cards and if so how many. A player may discard any number of cards that he chooses but most will exchange only one, two or three. No player of experience will exchange his entire hand, and there is little to be gained by retaining one card (a kicker) and exchanging four.

Further Betting

After the exchange of cards, he who was first to come in begins the betting. Either he throws in his hand (thereby sacrificing the stake he has already put up) checks (which means that he will remain in the game without increasing his stake) or raises by increasing his stake to any amount up to the agreed limit. If he checks those players who follow him have, each in his turn, the same choice. If no-one raises, those left in the game show their cards and the one with the best poker hand wins all that has been staked. If a player raises, the players who follow him have, each in his turn, the choice of either throwing in their hand, putting up sufficient money to meet the raise, or raising still further.

In this way the betting continues until the final bet is either called or not. If the bet is called, the players left in the game expose their cards and he with the best poker hand wins all that has been staked; if the bet is not called the player whose bet has not been called takes all that has been staked without need to show his cards.

Fundamentally, poker is a game of simple arithmetic. Suppose a player has been dealt:

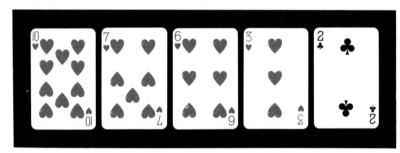

Many players will not hesitate to come in. They will discard ♣ 2 and ask for one card, hoping to draw a Heart to complete the flush. A pair of **10s** is of small value, so the only improvement is if a Heart is drawn. There are 47 cards from which to draw, and of these 9 are Hearts and 38 are not Hearts. It follows, therefore, that the odds against drawing a Heart are approximately $4\frac{1}{4}$ to 1. Now if two players have come in for 4 chips each, with the ante and straddle there will be 11 chips on the table. It will cost the player 4 chips to come in. The odds are not good enough to make it worth his while to do so, because the table is offering him only 11 to 4 or $2\frac{3}{4}$ to 1, and we have seen that his chance of improving is $4\frac{1}{4}$ to 1. If three players have come in for four chips each, it is still not worth his while coming in, because his chance of improving remains at $4\frac{1}{4}$ to 1 and the table is only offering odds of 15 to 4 ($3\frac{3}{4}$ to 1). Only if four players have come in for 4 chips each is it worth his while to come in, because now the table is offering odds of 19 to 4 ($4\frac{3}{4}$ to 1) which is rather better than his $4\frac{1}{4}$ to 1 chance of improvement. These calculations have to be made throughout the betting intervals.

This, then is the essence of good poker. What is the chance of improving my hand? What odds is the table offering me? If the former is greater than the latter you come in; if it is less you throw in your hand. Experienced players have the odds that the table offers them and the chances of improving a hand at their finger tips.

Chances of Improving
The importance of knowing what is the chance of improving a hand cannot be over emphasized. It is the most important factor in good play.

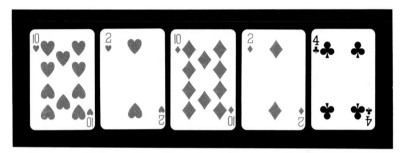

If ♣ **4** is discarded the odds against improving to a full house by drawing either a **10** or a **2** are about 11 to 1. The odds are the same against any improvement.

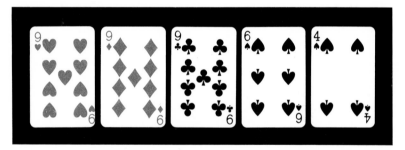

If ♠ **6 4** are discarded the odds against drawing ♠ **9** to make fours are about $22\frac{1}{2}$ to 1, the odds against drawing a pair, and so improving to a full house, are about $15\frac{1}{2}$ to 1, and the odds against making any improvement are about $8\frac{1}{4}$ to 1.

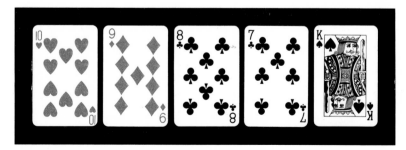

If ♠ **K** is discarded the odds against drawing a Jack or a 6, to improve to a straight, are about 5 to 1.

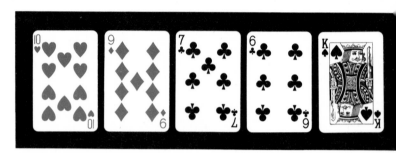

If the ♠ K is discarded the odds against drawing an 8, to improve to a straight, are about 11 to 1.

Finally:

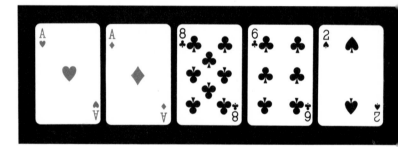

If ♣ 8 6 ♠ 2 are discarded the odds against drawing two Aces, to improve to fours, are about 359 to 1, against drawing three cards of the same rank, to improve to a full house, are about 97 to 1, against drawing one Ace, to improve to threes, are about 8 to 1, against drawing a pair, to improve to two pairs, are about 5 to 1, and the odds against making any improvement at all are about $2\frac{1}{2}$ to 1.

Pot-deals, commonly called Pots, are widely played because they add liveliness to what might otherwise be a rather dull game.

When a pot is played there is no ante and straddle. Instead, every player contributes an agreed amount (usually 2 chips) to a pot, or pool, that is independent of the stakes and betting.

The player on the immediate left of the dealer is first to decide whether to open the game by staking, or not. If he does not open, the option passes to the player on his left, and so on.

The most important feature of a pot is that a player may open the game, by putting up a stake, only if his hand qualifies him to do so because it conforms to a pre-arranged standard.

If no player opens the game the deal passes, and the players increase the amount in the pot (they are said to sweeten it) by contributing to it a further amount (usually agreed at 1 chip).

If a pot is opened, the other players may come in even though their hands are below the standard for opening it, and he who wins the deal wins not only the stakes put up by the other players, but also the amount in the pot.

A player is under no obligation to open even if his hand qualifies him to do so, but, after the hand has been played, the player who opened must show that his cards qualified him to open.

In a *Jackpot* a player must hold a pair of Jacks or better, to qualify for opening.

In a *Progressive Jackpot*, if no-one opens the first deal, the next is a Queenpot, and, if no-one opens it, it is followed by a Kingpot, and so on. Some stop at an Ace-pot; others continue to a Two-Pairs-Pot, before returning to a Jackpot.

In a *Freak-Pot*, or *Deuces Wild*, all the **2s** are wild cards and may be used to represent any card. In this event it is possible to have a hand of five of a kind (fives). It takes precedence over a straight flush, though in some circles it is inferior to a straight flush that is headed by the Ace (royal straight flush). It adds much to the excitement of the game, but the odds on improving a hand have to be calculated anew and are less reliable.

Stud Poker

Stud Poker is a variation of the parent game with the feature that some of the cards are dealt face upwards. There is no draw for fresh cards so that the game may be played by as many as ten.

There are several ways of playing the game. All are much of a muchness. In *5-Card Stud* there is no ante, unless by agreement. The dealer deals a card face downwards (it is known as a hole card) to each player, and then one card face upwards to each.

After looking at their hole cards the players bet on their combinations. He who has been dealt the highest face-upwards card makes the first bet, and if two or more players have equal cards the one nearest to the left of the dealer bets first. In the first betting interval this player must put up a stake (in later betting intervals the first bettor may check) and each player in turn· must either call the previous player or drop out of the game (fold).

After the round of betting, the dealer deals another card face upwards to all who remain in the game. There is another betting interval, the player with the highest exposed poker combination making the first bet. It should be noted, however, that straights and flushes do not count as poker combinations in this context, i.e., a player holding two cards of the same suit, and thus holding a possible flush, would not bet in advance of a player holding a pair or a card of a higher demonination.

This routine is repeated until every player has four face-up cards along with his hole card. After this round of betting if two or more remain in the game they expose their hole cards and he with the best poker hand wins the pot.

It is important that a player folds only in his turn. When he does so he turns face downwards all the face-up cards that have been dealt to him, and he must not expose his hole card.

It is the duty of the dealer to announce which hand is highest and which player, therefore, bets first. He should, for example, announce: 'Pair of Queens bets', and after the third and fourth card have been dealt he should also indicate a holding that may make a straight or flush; if the highest exposed combination is:

the dealer should announce: 'Possible flush'.

In all variations of poker bluffing plays an important part, though not such a big part as some may think. It necessitates that the game must be played for money, because any game that admits of betting in such a way as to give the impression that a hand is of value when, in fact, it is worthless makes nonsense if nothing concrete is at stake. Furthermore, if the game is to be worth while, the player must be prepared to risk as much as he can afford to lose. Poker becomes a pointless game, and one not worth playing, if the stakes are trivial in relation to the player's available resources.

Bezique

The game of bezique is for two players, playing with two packs of cards shuffled together, and from which the **6**s, **5**s, **4**s, **3**s and **2**s have been removed. The remaining cards rank: **A** (high) **10 K Q J 9 8 7**.

After shuffling the pack, each player lifts a part of it and exposes the bottom card of his cut. The lowest deals first. Thereafter they deal alternately. If both cut a card of equal rank they cut again.

Before the deal the cards are shuffled and cut by the non-dealer; the dealer completes the cut and deals eight cards to each player (beginning with his opponent) in bundles of three–two–three. The next card he exposes on the table and its suit determines the trump suit. The rest of the pack (the stock) is placed face downwards on the table, partly covering the exposed card.

The object of the game is to show and score for certain declarations, and to win tricks containing **Aces** and **10s**, known as brisques.

The players keep their scores on special markers, that take the form of clock-like indicators on thin cardboard. It is not practical to keep the score with pencil on paper.

If the dealer turns up a **7** as the trump card he scores 10 points. Thereafter, either player, after winning a trick, may exchange a trump **7** for the trump card, or declare a trump **7** for 10 points.

The non-dealer leads to the first trick; thereafter the player who wins a trick leads to the next. It is a feature of the game that a player is not compelled to follow suit to the card led: he may, if he prefers, discard on it or win it by trumping.

When a player wins a trick he may make a declaration by placing on the table, face upwards in front of him, those combinations of cards that score. The cards are left there until he decides to play them, and this he may do at any time.

The declarations, and scores for them are:

Double Bezique = 500 points. ♠ Q ♠ Q ♦ J ♦ J but if Spades or Diamonds are trumps ♣ Q ♣ Q ♥ J ♥ J
Sequence in Trumps = 250 points. **A 10 K Q J** of the trump suit
Any four Aces = 100 points
Any four Kings = 80 points
Any four Queens = 60 points
Any four Jacks = 40 points
Bezique = 40 points. ♠ Q ♦ J but if Spades or Diamonds are trumps ♣ Q ♥ J
Royal Marriage = 40 points. **K Q** of the trump suit
Common Marriage = 20 points. **K Q** of the same plain suit

These scores are recorded when the declaration is made.

A player may declare and show more than one declaration in a turn, but he may score for only one of them at the time; he must wait until he wins another trick before declaring another. For example, a player may expose ♠ K ♠ Q ♦ J and score for either the marriage or bezique not both; he must wait until he wins another trick before he may score for the other combination.

A card may not be used twice in the same declaration, but it may be used in different declarations. For example, the ♠ Q may be used in a marriage, sequence, bezique and four Queens, but if it has been used in a declaration of four Queens and one of them has been played, another Queen may not be exposed and four Queens again declared; four other Queens are necessary to score the 60 points.

The **K Q** of the trump suit may be declared as a royal marriage, and later the **A 10 J** may be added to score the sequence. If, however, the **A 10 K Q J** is first declared as a sequence, the **K Q** cannot be declared as a royal marriage. In the same way ♠ Q ♦ J may be declared as bezique and later the other ♠ Q ♦ J added to score for double bezique. If all four cards are declared together as double bezique, the player loses the 40 points for bezique.

When a player has won a trick, and made a declaration, if any, he takes into his hand the top card of the stock and the loser of the trick takes the next card of the stock. No declaration may be made, however, when the stock is reduced to one face-downwards card and the trump card.

The players now take into their hands any cards that they may have exposed on the table and play them out. The winner leads, and in this, the final stage of the hand, a player must follow suit if he is able to, and must win a trick if he is able to.

The player who wins the last trick scores 10 points, and the two players examine the tricks they have won and score 10 points for every brisque.

The game is won by the player who is first to reach 1,500 points, or the higher score if both players score 1,500 points in the same deal.

Rubicon Bezique

Rubicon bezique is very similar to the parent game, but with the advantage that it is governed by a code of laws drawn up by the Portland Club, London.

The chief differences between the two games are in the preliminaries, the scoring and the routine.

The game is played with four (not two) packs of cards. Each player is dealt nine (not eight) cards and no card is exposed to determine the trump suit. Trumps are determined by the first marriage or sequence to be declared.

The scoring is the same as that of the parent game, with the following additions:

Carte Blanche = 50 points. A player who is dealt no court card (**K Q J**) may score for carte blanche after showing his hand to his opponent. Then, each time that he draws a card from the stock, if it is not a court card, he may show his hand to his opponent and score 50 points
Ordinary Sequence = 150 points. **A 10 K Q J** of a suit other than the trump suit
Triple Bezique = 1,500 points
Quadruple Bezique = 4,500 points
Last Trick = 50 points

The tricks are left exposed on the table until a brisque is played. After this the tricks are gathered and turned in the usual way. The same cards may be used more than once in the same declaration, and if a player has declared two marriages in the same suit, he may rearrange the Kings and Queens and declare two more. Brisques are disregarded, except to break a tie or to save a player from being rubiconed. The game is complete in one deal, and the player with the higher score adds 500 points to it. If a player fails to score 1,000 points he is rubiconed: that is to say, his score is added to (not subtracted from) that of his opponent, who adds a further 1,300 points (not 500) to his total. Finally, if a player fails to win 100 points, the winner adds an extra 100 points to his total.

Six-pack or Chinese Bezique
Six-pack or Chinese Bezique is a very popular variation of the parent game, much enjoyed by Sir Winston Churchill who was an expert player of it. It is fast, high-scoring and exciting.

The player who cuts the higher card to determine the deal has the option of dealing or telling his opponent to do so. He will be advised to pass the deal to his opponent, because the dealer is at a disadvantage.

Before dealing, the dealer lifts a number of cards from the top of the pack. If the number of cards lifted is exactly twenty-four he scores 250 points. The non-dealer guesses the number of cards lifted, and if he guesses correctly he scores 150 points.

The dealer gives twelve cards to each player, starting with his opponent, singly and does not expose the next card to determine the trump suit. As in rubicon bezique, trumps are determined by the first marriage or sequence. The stock is placed face downwards between the two players, and toppled over to make drawing cards from it easier.

The declarations and the scores for them are:

Sequence in Trumps = 250 points
Sequence in a Plain Suit = 150 points
Royal Marriage = 40 points
Common Marriage = 20 points
Bezique = 40 points
Double Bezique = 500 points
Triple Bezique = 1,500 points
Quadruple Bezique = 4,500 points
Four Aces in the Trump Suit = 1,000 points
Four Kings in the Trump Suit = 900 points
Four Queens in the Trump Suit = 600 points
Four Jacks in the Trump Suit = 400 points
Any Four Aces = 100 points
Any Four Kings = 80 points
Any Four Queens = 60 points
Any Four Jacks = 40 points
Carte Blanche = 250 points

The non-dealer leads to the first trick; thereafter the winner of a trick leads to the next. It is not compulsory to follow suit to the card led. Points are not scored for brisques nor for winning tricks, so the played cards are not gathered and turned as tricks, but left face upwards in a heap on the table.

The winner of a trick may score for a declaration, and the same card may be counted more than once in a declaration. Only one declaration may be scored in one turn, but more than one declaration may be announced in one turn, and the player who has several declarations pending may choose the order in which he will score for them. All unscored declarations should be announced after every trick has been played, whether the trick has been won or lost.

No declaration may be scored after the last two cards of the stock have been drawn. The players pick up any cards they may have on the table and play off the last twelve tricks, following suit to the card led if able to do so, and winning the trick if possible.

There is no score for winning the last trick.

A game is complete in one deal. The player with the higher score is the winner, and adds 1,000 points to his score. A player who fails to score 3,000 points is rubiconed.

The same suit may not become trumps in two consecutive deals. A marriage in the trump suit for the previous deal may be declared, and 20 points scored for it, before the new trump suit is determined.

Pinocle

Pinocle (the name is sometimes spelt Pinochle, but the Oxford Dictionary does not sanction the H) is a game very similar to bezique. It originated in Europe but has never attracted English card players. It has, however, long since crossed the Atlantic where it is said to have a following of several million players. Originally a game for two players, American card players have developed a large number of variations, and to-day the most scientific and interesting is Auction Pinocle, a game that is unique first because it is a game for three players that is better when played by four; secondly because it is the only card game of skill that lacks a literature.

Auction Pinocle

In every deal only three players are active. If four play the dealer deals no cards to himself, and if five play he deals no cards to the player second to his left as well as none to himself. The inactive players, as they are called, take no part in the bidding and play, but participate in the settlement at the end of a deal.

The pack consists of forty-eight cards: the **A** (high) **10 K Q J 9** (in that order) of the four suits duplicated.

To determine seats and who shall deal first, the players draw cards from a pack spread-eagled on the table. If two or more draw cards of equal rank they draw again. The player who draws the lowest card has choice of seat and deals first. The player who draws the next higher card sits on his left, and so on. The deal rotates clockwise.

The dealer deals fifteen cards face downwards to each player in turn, beginning with the player on his left (eldest hand). The cards may be dealt either in three bundles of five each, or in three bundles of four each and one of three. After the first round of the deal, three cards are dealt face downwards on the table, in front of the dealer, as a widow-hand.

Each player in turn, beginning with the eldest hand, must either pass or make a bid. If a player passes he cannot re-enter the bidding. A bid is a contract to score, either by melds, by cards won in play, or by both, the number of points named. The eldest hand must open the bidding with a bid of at least 300, but in some circles it is reduced to 250. All subsequent bids must be in multiples of ten, and, of course, be for more than the previous bid. When two players pass a bid the bidding ends: the player who made the bid becomes the bidder, his bid the contract, and the two players who passed play in partnership as his opponents.

If the opening bid of 300 is passed by the other two players, the bidder may concede defeat without looking at the widow-hand. He throws in his cards, pays 3 units to a kitty (but nothing to his opponents) and the deal passes to the next player.

If, however, the bid is for more than 300, or if the bidder does not wish to concede defeat, he faces the widow-hand and may, if he wishes, take the cards into his hand. He then names the trump suit, and places face upwards on the table in front of him those melds that he wishes to declare.

The melds are scored for as follows:

Class A
A 10 K Q J of the trump suit = 150 points
K Q of the trump suit (royal marriage) = 40 points
KQ of a plain suit (common marriage) = 20 points

Class B
Pinocle (♠ **Q** and ♦ **J**) = 40 points
Dix★ (**9** of the trump suit) = 10 points

Class C
Four Aces (one of each suit) = 100 points
Four Kings (one of each suit) = 80 points
Four Queens (one of each suit) = 60 points
Four Jacks (one of each suit) = 40 points

No card may be used twice in melds of the same class, but the same card may be used in two or more melds of different classes.

Only the bidder has a right to meld. The other two players (who are partners against the bidder) agree with him upon the amount of his melds and the number of further points, if any, he needs to fulfil his contract, and the bidder then returns the melded cards to his hand.

Before play begins (preferably before the bidder picks up his melds) he must bury (discard) three cards from his hand in order to restore his hand to fifteen cards in all. He may bury any three cards that he chooses, except those that he has used in a meld. If, for example, the bidder has melded the ♠ **K Q** as a common marriage, he may bury neither card, but, of course, if he holds two Kings of Spades or two Queens of Spades he may bury one of them, but not both; and if he has used both Kings and both Queens in melds he

---

★Dix (pronounced dees) is the French word for ten. Pinocle-players sometimes spell it dis.

may bury none. The cards that the bidder buries need not be shown to the opponents. They should be placed face downwards on the table near the bidder because later they will be counted for him as a trick won.

The bidder leads to the first trick. Before he does so he may change, as often as he wishes, the trump suit, the melds and the cards he has buried. Once he has made the opening lead, however, he may make no changes.

If the bidder thinks that he will be unable to make his contract he has a right to concede defeat (called single *bête**). In this event, instead of leading a card, he throws in his hand and pays the others (active and inactive) the value of his bid.

When playing to a trick, a player must, if he can, follow suit to the card led: if he cannot he must play to win the trick by trumping it, but if a previous player has already trumped the trick he is under no compulsion to over-trump. Only if a player has no card of the suit led and no trump card may he discard a plain-suit card.

If a trump is led, each player in turn must play a higher trump than any already played to the trick. If he can follow suit, but cannot over-trump, he may play any trump.

A trick is won by the player who plays the highest card of the suit led or the highest trump. If two players play identical cards the card first played wins the trick.

The player who wins a trick leads to the next.

When all the tricks have been played, a player scores . . .

For every Ace won 11 points, every Ten 10 points, every King 4 points, every Queen 3 points, every Jack 2 points and for winning the last trick 10 points.

A simpler system of scoring is: For every Ace and Ten won 10 points, every King and Queen 5 points and for winning the last trick 10 points.

An even simpler system is: For every Ace, Ten and King won 10 points and for winning the last trick 10 points.

It will be seen that no matter which system is preferred, the total points to be won in every deal amounts to 250.

Every deal is a separate event, and at the end of each, before the next deal begins, the players—active and inactive—make settlement either in cash, with chips, or by recording on paper the wins and losses of the players.

*A French word that is pronounced bayt.

It is usual to reduce the contract to units, on which payment is made:

A CONTRACT of:	has a UNIT VALUE of:	
300–340	3	The unit values are doubled
350–390	5	if Spades are trumps.
400–440	10	
450–490	15	
500–540	20	
550–590	25	
600 and more	30	

Another schedule is:

300–340	1	The unit values are doubled
350–390	2	if Spades are trumps and
400–440	4	trebled if Hearts are
450–490	6	trumps.
500–540	8	
550–590	10	
600 and more, 2 units are	12	
added for each step of 50		
points.		

The bidder pays double (called double *bête*) if his score for melds and cards taken in tricks fails to equal his contract; he receives, but not more than the unit value of his contract, if his score equals or exceeds his contract.

Payment is made to and from all players, active and inactive, and if the contract is for 350 or more to and from the kitty.

The kitty is a separate account. As we have seen, it alone collects when a minimum bid of 300 is forfeited, and it pays or collects the same as an opponent when the bid is for 350 or more. The kitty is the common property of the players who must make good any deficiency if it owes, and divide any surplus when the game breaks up.

Auction pinocle is a game that, to play well, calls for as much technical knowledge and experience as any other scientific game of cards. As a result, it is essential to take it seriously; light-hearted play is to be frowned on.

Hand valuation is not difficult. The player counts the value of his melds and estimates the points he can win in tricks. He then takes into consideration the cards he needs to increase his melding and playing strength, and the probability of finding them in the widow-hand. Pinocle players use the term 'places open' to mean the number of cards needed to improve a hand. As there are two cards of every suit and of every rank in the pack the odds against finding a specified card in the widow-hand are 5 to 1 against if one place is open, 2 to 1 against if two places are open, evens if three places are open, 3 to 2 on if four places are open and 2 to 1 on if five places are open.

The two players in partnership against the bidder should bear in mind that there are three general rules of play that, if respected, will prove to their advantage in the long run. If the player on the left of the bidder leads an Ace, his partner should play on it the other Ace of the suit if he holds it. When a trick is won by one of the partners, the other should play a high-scoring card on it and keep in hand his low cards to play on tricks won by the bidder. The partner on the right of the bidder is advised to lead a trump when it is apparent that the bidder's trump suit is weak. As an aid to memory, these three rules of play are condensed to: 'An Ace calls for an Ace', 'Fatten partner's tricks' and 'Lead through a weak trump suit.'

Auction Pinocle for 1,000 Points
Among the many variations developed by American card players, Auction Pinocle for 1,000 points is to be recommended.

The game may be played either by three or four, but when four play the dealer receives no cards. The deal and bidding are conducted as in the parent game, but the lowest bid is for 100. The bidder faces the widow-hand, adds it to his own and names the trump suit. All the players then meld what they can. The bidder buries three cards (which must not include any card that he has melded) and leads to the first trick. The play is conducted as in the parent game.

Each player plays for himself and scores what he makes in melds and wins in tricks, but a player (other than the bidder) cannot score for his melds unless he wins at least one trick. The bidder need not win a trick to score his melds because the three cards that he has buried count as a trick for him.

If the bidder fails to score as much as he bid he is set back by the amount of his bid.

The game ends when a player has reached a total of 1,000 points. The bidder's points are counted first.

Piquet

Piquet (a French word, but pronounced as though English) is a game for two players and generally considered the best card game for two ever devised. It is played with what is known as the short pack, namely a pack of cards from which the **6**s, **5**s, **4**s, **3**s and **2**s have been removed. The remaining cards rank in the normal order from **Ace** (high) to **7** (low). The suits are of equal rank.

A *partie* (game) consists of six deals. The players draw cards to decide who shall deal first. The higher has choice and would be advised to take the deal because it gives a slight advantage. Thereafter the players deal alternately.

The dealer deals twelve cards to each player. The cards must be dealt either two or three at a time, at the choice of the dealer, who must not change the mode during the *partie*. He deals first to his opponent. The remaining eight cards (the stock) is placed face downwards on the table between the players, and it is customary that the top five cards are placed slightly apart from the other three.

The non-dealer (known as elder) has a right to discard five of his cards and refill his hand with the top five cards of the stock. He is not compelled to exchange five cards but he must exchange at least one. If he exchanges less than five cards he may look at those that he has not taken from the stock.

The dealer (known as younger) has a right to discard three of his cards and refill his hand with the bottom three cards of the stock. He is not compelled to exchange three cards but he must exchange at least one. If elder has not taken all his five cards, younger may take them. If any cards are left in the stock elder may look at them and, if he does, he must show them to younger. If elder does not look at them, younger may not.

The cards that have been discarded by the players should not be mixed, because during the play of the hand a player has the right to look at the cards that he discarded.

If a player has been dealt no King, Queen or Jack, he may show his hand to his opponent and score 10 points for *carte blanche*. A hand is shown by rapidly counting the cards in it face upwards on the table.

The object of discarding cards and filling the hand from those in the stock is to obtain certain scoring combinations, as listed below:

Point. The player with most cards of one suit scores as many points as he has cards in that suit. If both players have the same number of cards in their respective suits, the point is scored by the one with the greater pip value, counting the Ace as 11 and the court cards 10 each. If there is an equality of pips neither player scores.

Sequence. Three or more consecutive cards in a suit constitute a sequence. A sequence of three cards (tierce) scores 3 points, four (quart) 4 points, five (quint) 15 points, six (sixième) 16 points. seven (septième) 17 points and eight (huitième) 18 points. Only the player with the best sequence scores, and he scores for any other sequences that he may hold. Any sequence is higher than one of lesser length and if two or more sequences are of equal length the one headed by the highest card scores. If the players tie for best sequence, neither scores.

Quatorze and *Trio.* Any four cards of the same rank and higher than a 9 constitute a quatorze, and any three a trio. The player who holds the highest quatorze or trio scores it and any other quatorzes and trios that he may hold. Quatorzes score 14 points each, trios 3 points each. As between quatorzes and trios that highest in rank of cards scores.

On demand a player must show any combination of cards for which he has scored. In practice, however, it is rarely necessary for him to do so as an opponent is usually able to infer the suit of his opponent's point, sequence, quatorze or trio.

A player is under no compulsion to declare a combination that he holds. If he holds four Kings, for example, it is ethical to declare only three to mislead his opponent in the play. The practice is known as sinking.

The scores are called in the order: Carte Blanche (if any), Point, Sequence, Quatorze and Trio.

When elder has counted his hand, he leads a card and scores 1 point.

Younger now counts his hand and plays to the card led by elder.

The twelve tricks are played out. A player must follow suit to the card led if he is able to. The player of the higher card of the suit led wins the trick, and leads to the next. The player who leads to a trick scores 1 point. The opponent of the leader scores 1 point if he wins the trick. The winner of the last trick scores 1 point, and if a player wins more than six tricks he scores 10 points for the cards. If, however, a player wins all twelve tricks, he scores 40 points for *capot*, but does not score for the last trick nor for the cards.

If elder reaches a score of 30 points or more in declarations and play, and before younger has scored anything, he adds 30 points to his score for *pique*. If either player reaches a score of 30 points or more in declarations, before his opponent has scored anything, and before a card is led, he adds 60 points to his score for *repique*.

During the declarations and play of the cards, the score is kept verbally. Every time that a player scores he announces his cumulative total and repeats it when his opponent scores. At the end of each deal a note is made of the totals, and at the end of the *partie* the player with the higher total wins the difference of the totals plus 100 points for the *partie*, provided that his opponent has scored at least 100 points. If he has not, he is rubiconed, and the winner, whether his score reaches 100 or not, scores the sum of the two totals plus 100 points for the *partie*.

Gin Rummy

The game of Rummy is derived from the Spanish game of *Con quien?* (With whom?) corrupted into English as coon can. Many variations of the parent game are known. Canasta is one, but before canasta became fashionable, gin rummy had been popularized by the show-biz personalities of the 1930s, and to-day, played with the Hollywood scoring, it is one of the most popular of all card games.

Primarily the game is for two players, but three players (one playing against the other two playing in partnership) or four (two playing in partnership against the other two playing in partnership) may participate. The last is generally considered to make the best game.

The game is played with the full pack of fifty-two cards, ranking from **King** (high) to **Ace** (low). The players cut to determine who shall deal the first hand; thereafter the players do not deal alternately as in most games, but he who wins a hand deals the next.

The cards are dealt face downwards one at a time to each player, until each has received ten cards. The next card (known as the up-card) is placed face upwards in the centre of the table, and the rest of the pack (known as the stock) is placed face downwards alongside it.

The object of the game is to meld one's cards into a set of three or four of the same rank (e.g. ♥K ♣K ♠K or ♥9 ♦9 ♣9 ♠9) or into sequences of three or more consecutive cards of the same suit (e.g. ♥10 ♥9 ♥8 ♥7, or ♠K ♠Q ♠J) but a sequence of cards in which the highest is considered adjacent to the lowest (e.g. ♦A ♦K ♦Q or ♦2 ♦A ♦K) is disallowed. Sets and sequences must be independent of each other: that is, a player is not allowed to meld the same card into a sequence and a set.

The pone (non-dealer) has first choice of taking the up-card into his hand. If he does not, he must offer it to the dealer. If either player takes the up-card he must discard a card from his hand face upwards on the table. If neither player takes the up-card, the pone takes the top card of the stock into his hand and discards a card from his hand to cover the up-card. The dealer then has the option of taking into his hand either the top card of the stock or the card that the pone has discarded. When he has taken one of them into his hand, he must discard a card from his hand. The discards made by the players are placed one on top of the other, so that only the card immediately discarded can be seen, and the discard pile must not be examined by the players while the hand is in play.

Play continues in this way – each player in turn taking into his hand either the top card of the stock or the top card of the discard pile—until one of them elects to go down (called knocking) or until only two cards are left in the stock. Neither may be drawn, and if the player who draws the fiftieth card discards without knocking, the hand is declared a draw; neither player scores and the same dealer deals again.

The player who knocks must do so after drawing a card and discarding, and his unmelded cards must not exceed a total of 10 points—counting the court cards at 10 points each and the other cards at their pip values.

Unless a player has declared gin (i.e. knocked with all his ten cards melded) his opponent may reduce his loss by adding cards from his hand to the melds exposed by his opponent.

Pone (who has not declared gin) knocks with:

Dealer who has been left with:

♥ **10 5 4** ♦ **Q 10 8 3** ♣ **10** ♠ **K 4**

may meld his three **10**s, and further reduce his loss by adding the ♥ **5 4** and ♠ **4** to the pone's sequences, and the ♦ **Q** to his set of Queens. As already explained, he must not add the ♠ **K** to the pone's Spade sequence as the ♠ **A** ends the sequence.

The play of the hand now comes to an end, and the score is calculated and recorded as follows:

1) The unmelded cards of the players are totalled in order to determine their respective point-counts.

2) A player who has declared gin scores 25 points for doing so and adds to it the point-count of his opponent.

3) If gin has not been declared: if the point-count of the knocker is less than that of his opponent, the knocker scores the difference between the two point-counts; if the point-count of the knocker is

more than that of his opponent, or if the point-counts of the players are equal, the opponent of the knocker scores 20 points for undercutting and adds to it the difference (if any) between the two point-counts.

The score is kept in three columns. The first hand that a player wins is recorded in Column 1; the second hand that he wins is recorded in Columns 1 and 2; the third and subsequent hands that he wins are recorded in Columns 1, 2 and 3.

When the score of a player in a column reaches a total of 100 points or more, the column is closed. The winner of a column scores 100 points for winning it, and a further 20 points for every hand that he has won in excess of those won by his opponent. If, however, the opponent has won more hands than the winner of the column, the opponent scores 20 points for each hand that he has won in excess of those won by the winner of the column, and this score is deducted from that of the winner of the column.

If a player fails to score in any column he is said to be blitzed and the total score of the winner of the column is doubled. A player who has been blitzed in any column records his first, or second, winning score in the next column which has not been won.

The game comes to an end when all three columns have been won.

If a player wins all three columns his final score is determined by adding together the scores he has won in the three columns: if a player has won two columns (and his opponent, therefore, only one column) the final score is determined by adding together the scores made by the player in two columns, and subtracting the lower total of either player from the higher.

Gin Rummy for Three Players

The players draw cards from a pack spread-eagled on the table. The one who draws the highest card is said to be 'in the box', and he plays against the other two playing in partnership. Only one player of the partnership plays the cards. He may consult with his partner on the play, but the active partner has the final decision. When the active partner loses a hand, the idle partner takes his place. The two partners alternate each time that one loses a hand.

If the player in the box loses a game he pays both partners, and, of course, receives from both if he wins.

A player remains in the box until he loses a game. The partners then cut cards to decide which of them shall go into the box.

When two players have each lost a game in the box, the third player goes into the box.

Gin Rummy for Four Players
Two play in partnership against the other two playing in partnership. Two packs of cards are necessary, preferably of different colour or different design. The partners sit facing each other. Two separate games are played. For the first hand the dealers deal to the opponents on their right. Thereafter the players alternate opponents.

The game is played up to 150 points and only one score is kept for each partnership; the net result of the partnership counts as one hand and is entered on the score-sheet as in the two-handed game.

When one partner finishes his hand, he may inform the other partner of the result, but he may not otherwise advise his partner until his partner's opponent has knocked. The idle partner may then advise his partner how to play, and he may draw attention to any irregularities.

Patience Games

In America patience games are known as solitaires. It is a more appropriate name for them, because they are intended to be played solus, to while away the time, as Napoleon did during his exile at St Helena.

Many hundreds of these games are known. A few are played with three packs of cards; still fewer with four packs. They are not popular, because, even when played with the extra-small packs, especially made for patience players, they are cumbersome and generally unsatisfactory.

Most patience games are played either with one pack or two. Among the one-pack games the Demon (known in America as the Canfield) and the Klondike (in England usually called the Canfield) are particularly well known, and those of us whose card playing goes back 60 and more years may remember that just before the war of 1914 Poker patience was all the rage: matches were played, tournaments were held and even leagues were formed. Among the two-pack games, Miss Milligan has been immortalized by E. F. Benson, and, while awaiting the outcome of events, the late President Franklin D. Roosevelt relaxed with a game of Spider.

Golf

From the many one-pack games I give first place to Golf, because not only may it be played solus, against bogey so to speak, but competitively in several ways.

Deal five rows of seven cards each. For convenience the cards in the rows may overlap. Known as the links, it is shown in Figure 1.

The remaining 17 cards (the stock) are held in hand. The top card of the stock is played to the table: ♠ 10.

Only the bottom card of each column is available for play. The object of the game is to clear the links by building on the cards from the stock, either in upwards or downwards sequences regardless of suit, but no sequence can go above a King or below an Ace. On the ♠ 10, the play is: ♠ 9, ♥ 10, ♣ J, ♣ 10, ♦ 9, stop.

Now the next card from the stock is played, and cards from the links built on it. And so on, until all 17 cards from the stock have been played and built on. The number of cards left in the links is your score for the hole. The cards are now picked up, shuffled and re-dealt for the next hole.

Played competitively, each player has his own pack and plays the holes simultaneously. Before play begins, however, the players must decide whether to play a 9-hole or an 18-hole match, and whether

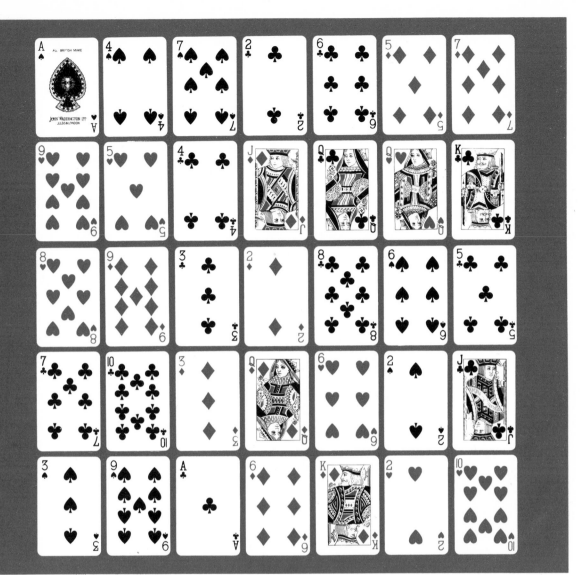

Fig. 1

they will determine the result by what golfers call match play or medal play. If a player clears the links before playing all the cards of the stock, the number of cards left in the stock count in his favour, and, at the end of the match, are deducted from the total score for his round.

Like golf itself, the game is ideally suited to two players, but with a little ingenuity three-ball matches and foursomes may be arranged. If played solus the bogey score is 4 for each hole.

Golfers confined to the club-house during an earthquake (if earthquakes confine golfers to the club-house) will find it a more engrossing game than bridge.

Grandfather's Clock

Grandfather's Clock is a one-pack patience, not too difficult and with an attractive lay-out (Figure 2).

Remove from the pack ♥ **2 6 10 ♠ 3 7 J ♦ 4 8 Q ♣ 5 9 K**,

Fig. 2

and arrange them in a circle comparable to the hours on the face
of a clock, with ♣ **9** at noon and the others in sequence round the
dial.

Counting the Jack as 11, the Queen as 12, the King as 13 and the
plain cards at their pip values, these foundation cards are built up
in suit sequences until they reach the number appropriate to their
positions on the dial. The sequence is continuous, with **Ace** above
King and below **2**.

The remaining 40 cards of the pack are dealt, face upwards, in
five rows of eight cards each (Figure 3). For convenience the cards
in the rows may overlap.

The cards in the bottom row are exposed. They may be built on
their appropriate foundation cards, or packed on other exposed

Fig. 3

cards in downwards sequences, regardless of suits. A space made by playing off a whole column may be filled by any available card.

The ♣ 10 is built on the ♣ 9, the ♦ K on the ♦ Q, and the ♣ A on the ♣ K. The ♠ 10 is packed on the ♦ J, the ♠ 6 on the ♦ 7, the ♠ 9 on the ♠ 10, and so on.

Two-pack Patiences

The result of nearly all games of patience is determined by luck– the fortuitous distribution of the cards. Two-pack patiences are no exception to the general rule, but, with twice the number of cards to control, they give the impression that the result depends on the skilful handling of the cards. As the majority of us like to think that we are thinking, two-pack patiences are very popular.

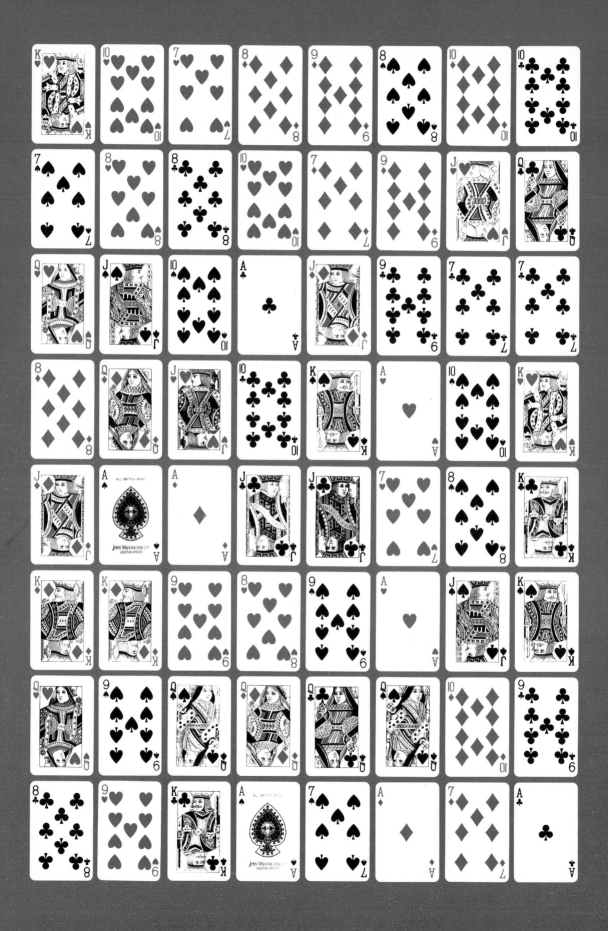

Persian

One of the best of the two-pack patiences is Persian, sometimes called Bezique, though why it should be is obscure.

The packs are stripped of the **2**s, **3**s, **4**s, **5**s, and **6**s, and the remaining 64 cards are shuffled together. They are then dealt out, face upwards, in eight rows of eight cards each (Figure 4). For convenience the cards in the rows may overlap.

Any **Ace** in the bottom row is played to the centre of the table as a foundation, to be built on in ascending suit sequence, the **7** following the **Ace**, up to the **King**.

The cards in the bottom row are exposed: they may be built on the Ace-foundations, or packed on other exposed cards in descending sequences of alternate colour.

A sequence may be moved only as a whole.

If a space is made, by taking all the cards from a column, any exposed card may be moved into the space and packed on.

When no further moves are to be made, the untaken cards are picked up, shuffled and re-dealt. Three deals are allowed, but if no cards can be taken after the first deal it does not count as one of the allowed three.

Play the ♠ **A**, ♦ **A** and ♣ **A** to the centre of the table. Build the ♠ **7** on the ♠ **A**, and the ♦ **7** on the ♦ **A**. Pack the ♣ **8** on the ♥ **9**, the ♦ **Q** on the ♣ **K**, the ♣ **9** on the ♦ **10**, and the ♠ **J**, ♦ **10** and ♣ **9** on the ♦ **Q**. Build the ♠ **8** on the ♠ **7**. Pack the ♥ **Q** on the ♠ **K**. And so on.

Fourteens Out

Fourteens Out is played with two full packs shuffled together. It is a good game for children, and some adults, because it keeps them out of mischief and teaches them to be alert to numbers.

The first 25 cards of the pack are dealt, face upwards, in five rows of five cards each (Figure 5). The remaining 79 cards (the stock) are retained in hand.

Counting the King as 13, the Queen as 12, the Jack as 11, and the plain cards at their pip value, remove any two cards in the same row or column that total 14. In the diagram the following pairs may be removed:

♦ **10** + ♠ **4**, ♦ **8** + ♦ **6**, ♣ **K** + ♦ **A** and ♣ **J** + ♥ **3**.

After removing a pair the vacant spaces are filled with cards from the stock.

When you are brought to a halt, you may interchange any two

Fig. 4

185

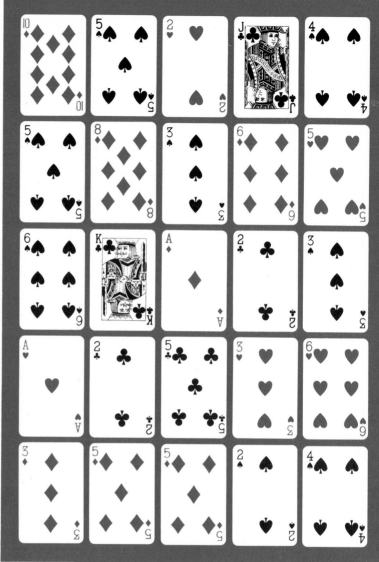

Fig. 5

cards, and when doing this naturally you will do so in a way as to obtain two fourteen-pairs and so give yourself four vacant spaces.

The object of the game is to clear all the cards from the table, and if the stock has been exhausted before this has been done, you take up the bottom row and fill the vacant spaces beginning at the top left-hand corner.

Continue until all or as many cards as possible have been paired off.

Patriarchs

Patriarchs is a two-pack patience with a similar lay-out to the better-known Sultan. It is, however, a rather more difficult game.

One Ace and one King from each suit are removed from the pack; the **Aces** are placed in a column to the left of the table, the **Kings** in a column to the right. They are the foundation cards.

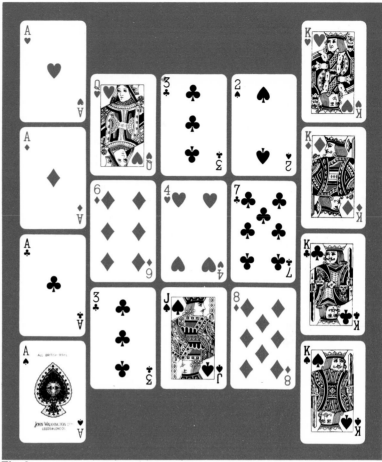

Fig. 6

Between them nine cards are dealt in three rows of three cards each to form the reserve (Figure 6).

The object of the game is to build suit-sequences, on the Aces up to the Kings and on the Kings down to the Aces. When the top cards of two foundation-piles of the same suit are in sequence, any or all of the cards of one pile (except the Ace or King at the bottom) may be reversed onto the other.

The cards in the reserve are available for play to the foundations. In the illustration, therefore, the ♥ Q is built on the ♥ K, and the ♠ 2 on the ♠ A. A space in the reserve must be filled at once from the waste-heap, or, if there is none, from the cards in hand (stock).

The cards in the stock are turned one at a time and any card that cannot be played to a foundation (or is not needed to fill a space in the reserve) is played to a waste-heap. When all the cards in the stock have been played, the waste-heap is picked up and dealt, but only once.

Gambling Games

Roulette, Craps—Peter Arnold

Roulette

Roulette is a gambling game of chance, in which the winning and losing is decided by a ball falling into a numbered pocket on a wheel which spins in one direction while the ball rolls in the other. Although no skill is required to play it, it has a fascination for games players with a liking for arithmetic because of the ingenuity of the systems which gamblers have invented for years in an effort to make their fortunes. The search for an infallible system continues despite periodic and mistaken claims that it has been found. Roulette is primarily a casino game, but home sets are marketed widely, and it is possible to hire full-size wheels and tables.

The use of a pocketed wheel and a ball for gaming dates back to about the year 1700 when a game called hoca became popular in casinos on the continent of Europe. In England a game called E.O. was played in which, instead of numbered compartments, all the pockets were lettered E or O (for even or odd). A game more similar to modern roulette was developed in Europe in the eighteenth century. Called boule, and still played today, it consists of a stationary wheel set in a bowl around which a ball is rolled. There are eighteen pockets numbered 1 to 9, two pockets for each number. Gamblers can back any number to win (and be paid 7 to 1 if successful), or back various groups of four numbers at even money. The number 5 is always a loser on these even-money bets. The bank thus can expect to retain over 11 per cent of all money staked, a much worse proposition for the gambler than playing roulette.

Roulette itself has also been played since the eighteenth century, and became very fashionable towards the end of the nineteenth, when the casino at Monte Carlo began to flourish and receive patronage from the royal families of Europe.

The Equipment

The basic equipment for roulette consists of the wheel and ball, and the table on which the bets are made. The wheel used in the Monte Carlo casino (Figure 1) has 37 pockets, numbered 1–36 and 0 (zero). The pockets are alternately red and black, except the zero pocket which is green. The numbers are arranged so that the high and low numbers, and the odd and even numbers also alternate as far as possible. In American casinos, the wheel is different (Figure 2). It has an additional zero pocket, numbered 00. As will be seen later, the effect of this extra pocket is to make betting on roulette much less attractive in American casinos than elsewhere, where a single zero is used. The arrangement of the numbers is

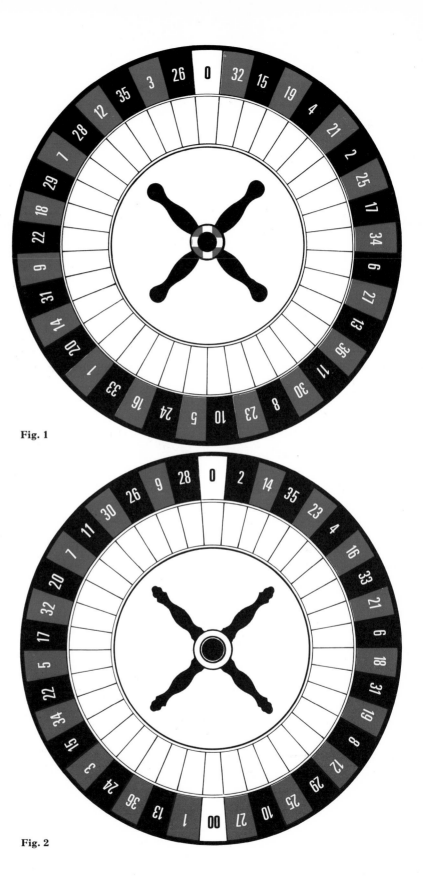

Fig. 1

Fig. 2

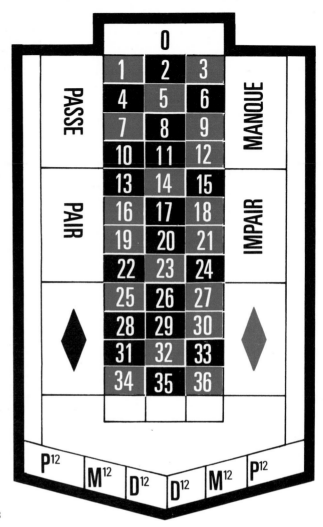

Fig. 3

different on the American wheel, although the eighteen red numbers on the Monte Carlo wheel are also red on the American wheel.

The table is of green baize cloth, marked in red, black and gold, although again the conventional layout differs in Monte Carlo and America. The layout of the table has no effect on the game, and indeed in Britain, where the Monte Carlo wheel is used, the table found in many casinos will be of the American pattern (but without the 00 space). The Monte Carlo table is illustrated in Figure 3 and the American table in Figure 4. The table in casinos might be double-ended, i.e. there will be a staking layout each side of the wheel, the zero being closest to the wheel at each end. The double-ended table allows more players to make bets in comfort.

The Casino Game
In a casino, roulette will be operated by croupiers, who will spin the wheel, rake in losing bets and pay out the winners. Bets will be made with the casino chips, which will usually be of a different colour for each player. When a game is in full swing, the wheel will be spun approximately every two minutes. Soon after setting the

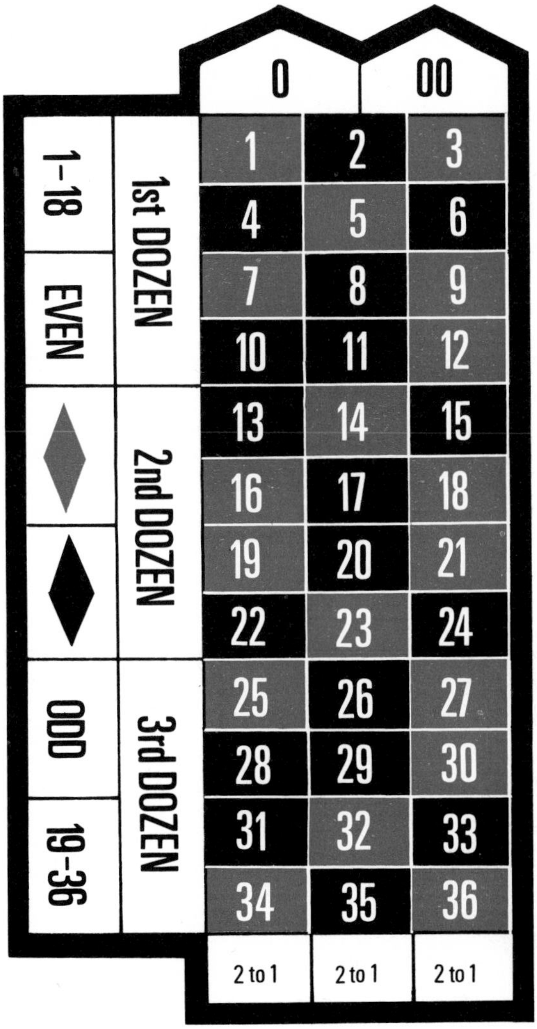

Fig. 4

wheel and ball in motion the croupier will call '*Rien ne va plus*' and no more bets may be made on that spin. The French language is traditionally used in describing roulette, although in English-speaking countries and particularly America this custom might not be observed, and '*Rien ne va plus*' becomes 'No more bets'.

The bets allowed fall into two categories, the even-money bets and those offering other odds.

The even-money bets are as follows:
Rouge, which is a bet that a red number will win
Noir, which is a bet that a black number will win
Pair, which is a bet that an even number will win
Impair, which is a bet that an odd number will win
Manque, which is a bet that a low number, 1–18, will win
Passe, which is a bet that a high number, 19–36 will win.

The stake is placed on the appropriate place on the table layout.
A player making a successful bet on one of these combinations will win an amount equal to his stake. An important difference

between European and American casinos arises regarding these bets. In most European casinos, should zero turn up, the stake is not automatically lost. It is put 'in prison' and remains on the table for another spin. Should the bet win on the second spin, the player is allowed to retain his stake, but does not collect any winnings. This is equivalent to the player losing half his stake should zero turn up, and in some casinos he may be allowed to withdraw half his stake and forfeit half. In American casinos, the bet will automatically be lost should zero or double-zero win. This convention puts the American gambler at a considerable disadvantage compared to the European gambler.

The other bets are as follows:

En plein (straight). This is a bet on a single number, and the stake is placed on the number on the table. It is allowable to bet on zero, and, on the American wheel, the double-zero. The odds paid are 35−1. The American gambler is still at a disadvantage since whereas the true odds are 36−1 on the European wheel, they are 37−1 on the American wheel, there being an extra pocket. The same disadvantage applies to the remaining bets.

A cheval (split). This is a bet on two adjacent numbers on the table layout (not adjacent numbers on the wheel), and the stake is placed on the line between the two numbers. Zero or double-zero can be combined with a number adjacent to it. The odds paid are 17−1.

Transversale pleine (street). This is a bet on any three numbers in a horizontal line on the table, such as 22, 23, 24. The stake is placed on the outer line of the row. Zero or double-zero may be combined with any two adjacent numbers by placing the stake on the corner common to the three numbers. The odds paid are 11−1.

En carré (square). This is a bet on a block of four numbers forming a square on the table, such as 13, 14, 16, 17. The stake is placed on the corner common to all four numbers. Zero in Europe can be backed in conjunction with 1, 2, 3 by placing the stake on the outside corner common to the zero and the row 1, 2, 3. The odds paid are 8−1.

Transfersale simple or *sixaine* (line). This is a bet on six numbers comprising two horizontal rows, such as 31, 32, 33, 34, 35, 36.

The stake is placed on the outer corner common to the two rows. It is impossible to include the zero or double-zero in a *transversale simple*. The odds paid are 5−1.

Colonne (column). This is a bet on one of the three vertical columns of twelve numbers on the table. The stake is placed in the blank box at the foot of the column on the Monte Carlo table. On the American table (Figure 4) the three columns are marked '2−1', and these are the odds paid.

Colonne à cheval (split column). This is a bet on two adjacent columns, the stake being placed on the line between the two boxes at the foot of each. The odds paid are 2−1 on, or 1−2.

Douzaine (dozen). This is also a bet on twelve numbers. The alternatives are the low numbers, 1−12, the middle numbers, 13−24 or the high numbers, 25−36. The stake is placed on the Monte Carlo table on P (première) for 1−12, on M (moyenne) for 13−24, or D (dérnière) for 25−36. On the American table, the stake is placed on 1st Dozen, 2nd Dozen or 3rd Dozen respectively. The odds paid are 2−1.

Douzaine à cheval (split dozen). This is a bet on any two adjacent dozens, the stake being placed on the line between the appropriate two boxes on the table. The odds paid are 2−1 on, or 1−2.

In the casino game, the odds offered for each bet ensure an advantage to the casino. Where a wheel with one zero is used, and bets on even-money chances are placed in prison when zero wins, as in Europe, the casino will expect, in the long run, to win 1·35 per cent of all money staked on even money bets, and 2·7 per cent on all other bets. In American casinos, with a wheel with two zeros, and no in prison rule, the casino will expect to win 5·26 per cent of all stakes. The casino will impose a minimum and maximum stake for all bets.

The Private Game
When roulette is played privately, the bets and odds are exactly the same as in the casino game. This means that in most cases, the bank will show a profit at the end of the session. It may be that the host, or the supplier of the equipment, will take on the role of the bank,

in which case he will expect to win. However, it is possible for all players to share the bank, thus giving each an equal chance of winning or losing.

The way to do this is for each player to contribute an equal amount before play begins to the bank. The total sum contributed forms the bank's capital. At the end of the game the money remaining in the bank is divided equally among the players. Since the bank expects to win, this will usually be more than the amount contributed.

It may be, of course, that not every player will wish to share in the bank. In this case, players may have unequal shares in the bank. For ease of calculation let us say there are ten players. Fix the bank's capital as 1,000 units (which might be £10 or £100, or $1,000), and offer each player 100 units. Say only six players wish to have a share in the bank, and all take 100 shares. This leaves 400 shares over. If all six players would like further shares in the bank, then lots may be drawn to decide which four may purchase a second hundred shares. The total of 1,000 shares, and the lots of 100 per player, are suggested so that the ultimate sharing-out of the bank's capital becomes easier. For example, if the capital in the bank at the end of the game is 4,200 units, each holder of 100 shares receives 420 units in the share-out. Another system is to allow each player to buy as many shares as he likes, up to a maximum. The only disadvantage is that if the total shares taken are, say, 730, the final sharing-out will involve awkward fractions.

If during the course of the game the bank runs out of capital, then the players holding shares must replenish it by the same amount as their original shares.

As in the casino game, minimum and maximum stakes should be set. The following table suggests minimums and maximums in units.

	Minimum	Maximum	Odds
En plein (single number)	1	2	35–1
A cheval (two numbers)	1	4	17–1
Transversale plein (three numbers)	1	6	11–1
En carré (four numbers)	1	8	8–1
Transversale simple (six numbers)	1	12	5–1
Colonne and Douzaine (twelve numbers)	2	25	2–1
Even-money and other bets	4	100	

The game would operate more conveniently if counters were

Roll	Winning Number	Colour	Odd or Even	High or Low	Columm	Dozen
1	3	R	O	L	3	1
2	17	B	O	L	2	2
3	8	B	E	L	2	1
4	14	R	E	L	2	2
5	36	R	E	H	3	3
6	0	–	–	–	–	–
7	9	R	O	L	3	1
8	17	B	O	L	2	2

Fig. 5

used as stakes rather than currency. Four colours might be used, to represent one, two, five and ten units. There should be a good supply of counters, so that players running out during the game may purchase more. All money collected for counters, including those forming the bank should be kept to one side. At the end of the game, when the counters in the bank have been distributed among the shareholders, all players cash in their counters.

It is an advantage if one member of the party, instead of playing, acts as banker and croupier. If the party plays regularly, the banker might be decided by rotation. Should nobody be willing to perform this task, then one of the players may look after the bank, but he must be careful to keep his own capital and the bank's separate. If the banker plays, the game will be slowed down.

A fixed period of play should be agreed beforehand. This prevents embarrassment should some players wish to stop when others wish to continue. If about four hours is agreed for the session, then it might be divided into two halves of 50 spins each, with an interval for refreshment. The host should prepare a ruled sheet of paper with 100 lines numbered 1–50 and 51–100, with three columns for each line. After each spin he should enter in the columns the winning number, the colour, and whether it is odd or even. This will ensure that the agreed number of spins are made, and it will enable system players to check the sequences. If the players wish it, three additional columns might be added to indicate whether the winning number is high or low or in which column or dozen it is contained. Figure 5 shows the beginning of such a full chart. It is because the croupier has to spin the wheel, settle the bets, keep the chart and generally see that the game proceeds properly, that it is advised that he should not play himself.

Systems
For games players who prefer their fortunes to depend on skill, or skill allied to chance, rather than on chance alone, the pleasure of roulette comes from an appreciation of staking systems, and the invention or choice of a plan and putting it into operation.

It is impossible, of course, to devise a system which will guarantee to win. On every bet made at roulette, the bank enjoys an advantage of at least 1·35 per cent, and no clever manipulation of numbers is going to alter that.

The best known and simplest of all staking systems is the martingale, or 'doubling-up' system. It is used on the even-money bets, as listed above. The player stakes one chip on, say, red. If it loses he doubles his stake and his next bet is two chips. Another loss and he stakes four chips. Eventually, he will win, and when he does his win will equal all his previous losses plus one chip. Since ultimately a win is a certainty, the system cannot lose. However, the 1, 2, 4, 8, 16 progression very rapidly reaches large numbers. After ten successive losses, the player has already lost 1023 chips and must stake 1024 on the next spin. Red once came up 28 times running at Monte Carlo, so even a Rockefeller, had he been backing black, would have needed to send for more funds. In practice, of course, a run of losers soon necessitates a stake above the maximum allowed, so the martingale is unworkable.

The system is more fun played in reverse. Instead of doubling losing stakes, winnings can be left on the table to double, and will mount as quickly as the stake does in the martingale system. If it is decided to collect the winnings only after eight successive wins, the number of chips taken will be 256. And as the stake is never more than one chip, it will take a long time to pay back 256 chips.

Another popular system is to increase the stake by a chip after a loss, and to decrease it by one after a win. The idea, as with the martingale, is to have the larger stakes on the winners, and if winners and losers alternate there will be one chip more on each winner than each loser. Unfortunately sequences are never as neat as that, but the system has the merit of keeping stakes within reasonable limits.

There are fewer systems for backing single numbers, and they usually rely on the fallacious 'law of averages'. The most popular is backing 'sleepers', which are numbers which have not won for some time and are consequently considered 'due'. A number can be expected to win, on a 37 number wheel, once in 37 spins on average. The *systémier* waits until a number has not appeared for 111 spins (3×37) and then backs it 37 times with a single stake, then increases the stake to two chips, and after a further 37 spins to three chips. The theory is that numbers rarely sleep for as many as 222 spins, but it will be noticed that the system does not necessarily show a profit when the expected win comes. In any case, the system is based on the premise that past results will affect future ones, which on a fair wheel is clearly erroneous.

A more valid system, perhaps the most interesting of all, is another based on the even chances, the 'cancelling-out' system. The player begins by writing down a short series of numbers, say

1, 2, 3, 4 or 2, 2, 2 or 1, 1, 2, 2. He backs one of the even money chances, and his first stake is the sum of the two outside numbers of his series. Were the series 1, 1, 2, 2, his first stake would be $1 + 2 = 3$. Should he win, he cancels the two outside numbers, leaving his series as 1, 2. His stake is therefore again 3, and should he win again his whole series is cancelled, and he is six units to the good. Should his second bet lose, he adds the losing stake, 3, to his series, which becomes 1, 2, 3 and his next stake is again the sum of the outside terms, in this case $1 + 3 = 4$. The beauty of the system is that every time the player wins, he cancels two numbers in his series, and every time he loses he adds only one, so that his series will always ultimately be cancelled out. And every time it is, he will win the sum of the numbers in his series – in the example followed, six units. The system's only drawback is that when a long adverse sequence occurs the stake can mount quickly.

The variety of roulette bets allows the player to invent systems as simple or complicated as he pleases. It will be noticed, for instance, that the third column on the roulette table contains eight red numbers and only four black. Suppose the player backs this column at odds of 2-1. He can expect to lose roughly twice for every win, but he can hedge his bet by also backing black. If his column bet wins, he must win at least one chip overall, perhaps three. When his column bet loses, his bet on black stands a better than even chance of saving his total stake, because there are 14 possible black winners in the first two columns to only ten reds. The backer has 26 of the 37 numbers on his side. It sounds an attractive plan, but it is a snare. The column bet will lose one chip in 37 to the bank, the bet on black one chip in 74, and there is no way of adding the two losses together to make a win.

Although the advantage in roulette must always be with the bank, the game is an enjoyable way to lose money, and serious students get their pleasure from the never-ending search for a plan which offers the promise of a good win with minimal losses.

Craps

Craps is a gambling game played with two dice, perhaps the oldest of all gambling implements. Early dice players used astragals, the ankle bones of cloven-footed animals (usually sheep), which have distinct faces. The modern game of craps developed during the twentieth century from an old English game called Hazard, which was popular all over Europe (but was not the game Chuck-a-Luck, which is sometimes called Hazard). Craps is now the most popular dice game, and in Las Vegas, the gambling capital of the world, the craps tables usually are the busiest. It is also the gambling game with the fastest 'action'.

Craps can be played either in casinos or privately. In casinos there will be a staking table (of about 10 feet by five feet) and the game will be operated by employees. All bets will be made against the bank. In private games, the only equipment necessary is the dice, and bets will be made amongst the players. In private games, therefore, the range of bets allowed will normally be smaller than that in casinos, and the odds paid for each bet will also differ, since there is no need to build in a percentage profit for the casino. The casino game will be described first, as it is the more complicated. In this article all numbers which represent a total thrown by the dice are printed in red.

Casino Craps
Craps in a casino will be played on a table like that in Figure 1. There are many different styles of layout, but that in the illustration is typical, and will serve to describe the bets. Seated at the centre

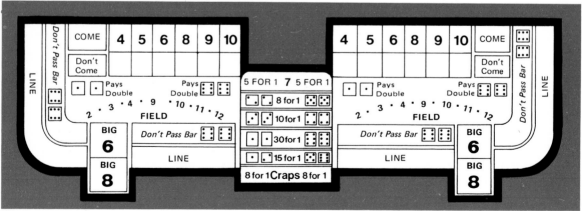

Fig. 1

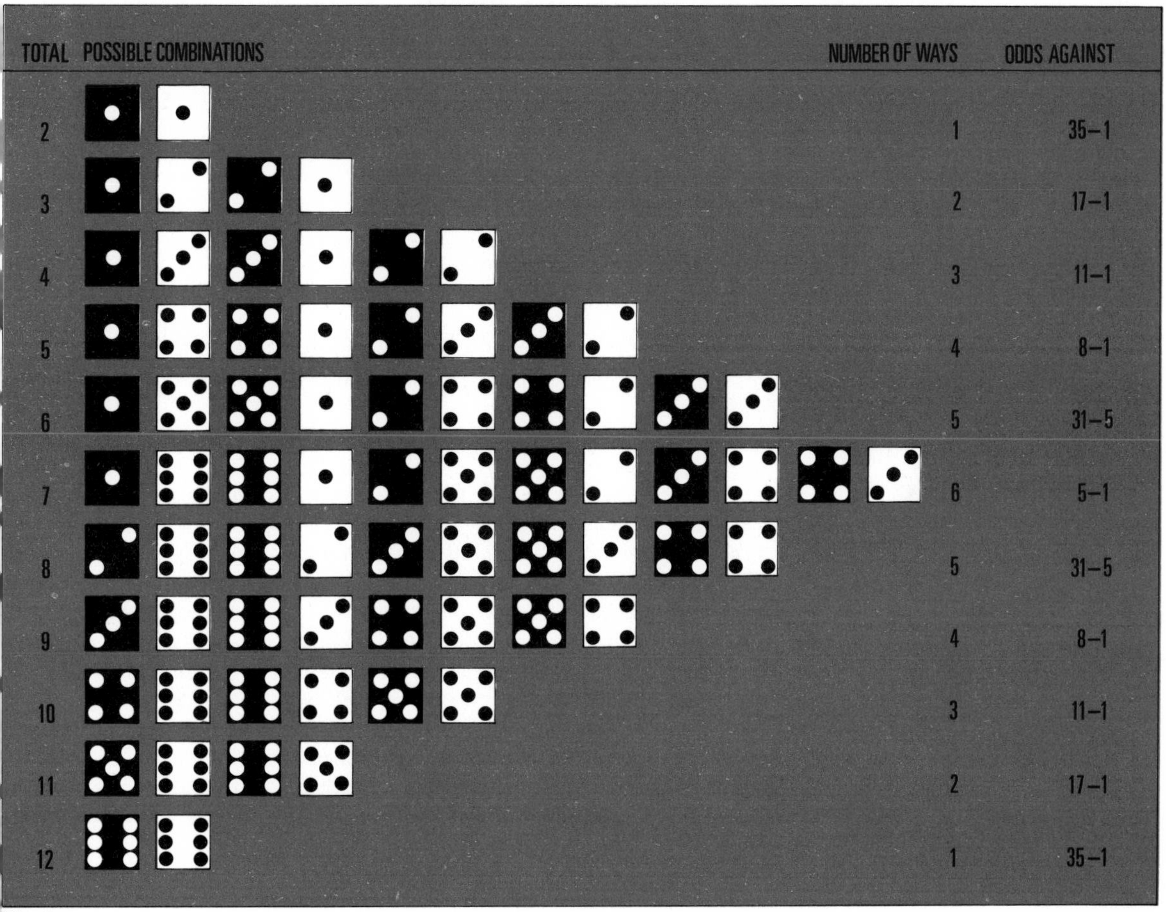

TOTAL	POSSIBLE COMBINATIONS	NUMBER OF WAYS	ODDS AGAINST
2		1	35–1
3		2	17–1
4		3	11–1
5		4	8–1
6		5	31–5
7		6	5–1
8		5	31–5
9		4	8–1
10		3	11–1
11		2	17–1
12		1	35–1

Fig. 2

12

of the table (at the top in the diagram) will be the boxman, who controls the game and keeps watch on all transactions. Opposite him will be the stickman who handles the dice and looks after the betting on the centre section of the table. On each side of the box-man will be a dealer, who looks after all bets at his end of the table. The gamblers stand round the table to left and right of the stickman, and use the casino's chips, which will usually vary in colour with the denomination.

The player who throws the dice is the shooter. He rolls the dice across the table so that they hit a backboard (which surrounds the table) before coming to rest. The first roll is known as his 'come-out' roll. The totals 7 and 11 are 'naturals', and should either be thrown the shooter wins immediately. The totals 2, 3 and 12 are 'craps', and mean the shooter loses. Should any other total appear it becomes the shooter's 'point', and the dealers at each end of the table place a marker in the box containing that number. The shooter then continues to roll the dice in an attempt to throw his point before he throws a 7. If he throws his point, he wins; if he throws a 7 he loses. Other totals do not count. A 7 therefore is a natural and a winner on the come-out roll, but a loser thereafter. Should the shooter win, the dice are said to 'pass' and a bet on this is called a 'right' bet. It is possible to bet that the dice 'don't pass' or 'miss-out', and this is a 'wrong' bet.

On this simple base is built a complex betting structure. However, the game remains one of chance only, and its main attraction to games players lies in examining the probabilities concerning the outcome of throwing two dice and comparing them with the various odds offered against the bets allowed. Figure 2 shows the 36 ways a pair of dice may fall, and lists the true odds against any total appearing. There are eight ways in which a shooter may come out with a natural 7 or 11, so that in the long run twice in every nine rolls the shooter will win immediately. There are a total of four ways in which the come-out roll may be a crap 2, 3 or 12, a loser for the shooter on one roll in nine. On the remaining six rolls in every nine, the shooter will make a point, and his chance of winning will vary with his point. To discover the shooter's overall chance of winning, a total of 1980 rolls must be considered to avoid fractions. Table 1 summarizes these rolls.

Table 1: Shooter's Probability of Passing

Come-out roll	Number of times thrown	Number of winning coups	Number of losing coups
2 crap	55	—	55
3 crap	110	—	110
4 point	165	55	110
5 point	220	88	132
6 point	275	125	150
7 natural	330	330	—
8 point	275	125	150
9 point	220	88	132
10 point	165	55	110
11 natural	110	110	—
12 crap	55	—	55
Totals	1980	976	1004

Thus, in the long run, of every 1980 come out rolls, the shooter will win 976 and lose 1004, and since the bank offers even money for a pass bet, it will enjoy an advantage over the shooter of 1·414 per cent.

Using the table above, it is possible to calculate the bank's percentage advantage in all the craps bets it will allow.

The bets and advantages are as follows:

Win, Do, Pass or Front Line. This is a bet that the shooter will pass, and the stake is placed on the space marked 'line' on the table. This line might on other tables be marked 'pass line' or 'win'. The odds offered are even money. As calculated above, the bank's advantage is 1·414 per cent.

Lose, Don't, Don't Pass or Back Line. This is a bet that the shooter will lose, and the stakes are placed on the 'Don't Pass' space. The odds are again even money. As there are more ways in which the shooter can lose than win, the bank must adjust the bet to retain its advantage. The 'Don't Pass' line in Figure 1 states the adjustment: 'Bar 6, 6'. This means that if the shooter comes out with a double-6, don't pass bets are void, and await a further throw. A double-6 will occur 55 times in the total of 1980 rolls listed in Table 1, and if these are barred, the shooter can lose only 949 times, while still winning 976 times, so the don't pass bettor finds that the casino keeps its advantage, although it is slightly less, 1·403 per cent. Some casinos bar double-1 rather than double-6, and their advantage remains the same. Others bar 1, 2, which occurs twice as often as double-1 or double-6, and their advantage rises to 4·385 per cent.

Come. This is a bet made when the shooter has already established his point. It is the same as a pass bet, except that the shooter's next roll will be considered as his come-out roll. The stake is placed in the box marked 'come'. If the shooter's next roll is a natural, the come bettor wins immediately. Similarly he loses if the next roll is a crap. Alternatively, the next roll might establish a point for the come bettor, in which case the dealer will move the stake to the appropriate point box. The bet is then the same as a pass bet, except that the shooter and the come bettor will have different points and will win or lose at different times in the sequence of rolls. The odds offered are even money. The bank's advantage is, as for pass bets, 1·414 per cent.

Don't Come. This bet is the opposite of a come bet, made when the shooter has established his point. As with a don't pass bet, the double-6 is barred (or the double-1 or 1, 2 as explained earlier). The don't come stake is placed in the box marked 'don't come', and

15

moved by the dealer to the blank square below the appropriate point square when the shooter has made a new point for the don't come bettor. The odds offered are evens. The casino's advantage is 1·403 per cent (or 4·385 per cent if the 1, 2 is barred).

Big Six and Big Eight. These are bets that a 6 or an 8 will appear before a 7, and the stakes are placed in the appropriate box. Reference to Figure 2 shows that a 7 will be thrown six times to every five for a 6 or an 8. The odds offered are even money, so the bank enjoys an advantage of 9.091 per cent.

Field. This is a bet that any of a group of numbers will appear on the next roll. The stake is placed on the space marked 'Field' on the table. The group of numbers on the table in Figure 1 is 2, 3, 4, 9, 10, 11, 12. Figure 2 shows that one of this group will appear 16 times in 36. The odds offered are even money, but to give the bettor a fairer bet, the double-6 and double-1 are paid double, i.e. at odds of 2−1. This means that the bettor on the field can expect a return of 34 chips for every 36 staked, an advantage to the bank of 5·556 per cent. The field varies, and some casinos will offer the 5 instead of the 4 in the field, but will not pay double on the double-1 and double-6. The bank's advantage remains the same.

Hardway. This is a bet that 4, 6, 8 or 10 will be made the hard way, i.e. by means of a double, before it is made any other way or before a 7 is thrown. The bets are placed in the appropriate place in the centre of the table, where it will be seen that the bank offers 8 *for* 1 (7 *to* 1) on hardway 4s and 10s, and 10 *for* 1 on hardway 6s and 8s. Since there are eleven ways in which a 6 or 7 can be thrown, and only one is a double-3, the correct odds for a hardway 6 are 10−1. In offering 10 *for* 1, the bank thereby takes an advantage of 9·091 per cent, and takes the same for hardway 8s. The bank's percentage on hardway 4s and 10s is 11·111 per cent.

Place or Box Numbers. These are bets that a chosen number will be thrown before a 7. Stakes are placed on the line above or below the respective point number. On 4 and 10 the bank pays odds of 9−5. Reference to Figure 2 shows the correct odds to be 2−1, so the bank's advantage is 6·667 per cent. On 5 and 9 the bank pays 7−5, its advantage being 4·000 per cent. On 6 and 8 the bank pays either 7−6, in which case its advantage is 1·515 per cent, or even money in which case its advantage is 9·091 per cent. Note that if the casino offers odds of 7–6 on place 6 and 8 bets, it is pointless backing Big Six and Big Eight at even money, where the bank enjoys nearly six times the advantage.

Buy or Lay Bets. A buy bet is similar to a place bet in that the player bets that a point number will appear before 7. The difference is that on the buy bet the casino will pay winners at the correct odds: for points 4 and 10 at 2–1, for 5 and 9 at 3–2, and for 6 and 8 at 6–5. However, it will exact a commission of 5 per cent of the stake. Since the minimum commission will be the minimum stake, the gambler must stake 20 times the minimum or pay a higher percentage commission. The casino's advantage on these bets is 4·762 per cent. Reference to the percentages for place bets shows that the player does better to buy bets on 4 and 10 and to place them on 5, 6, 8 and 9. Lay bets are the opposite of buy bets, i.e. the player bets that 7 appears before the point. The true odds are paid: for points 4 and 10 at 1–2, for 5 and 9 at 2–3, and for 6 and 8 at 5–6. The 5 per cent commission is this time exacted on the winnings rather than the stake, i.e. 1 chip commission will be levied on a stake of 40 on points 4 and 10, 30 on points 5 and 9, and 24 on points 6 and 8, since each of the bets will win 20 chips. The casino's advantage is respectively 2·439 per cent, 3·226 per cent and 4·000 per cent. The bets are made by the player placing his stake on the table and calling the point he wants. The dealer removes the house commission (called 'vigorish') from the stake and places the stake in the correct box.

Other Bets. There are various other bets or combinations of bets possible at craps. A few are shown on the table in Figure 1. Most are 'one-roll action' bets, and are settled on the result of one roll. For instance, a gambler can back 7 to appear on the next throw. The odds are 5 *for* 1, and the bank's advantage 16·667 per cent. Odds of 30 *for* 1 are offered for double-1 and double-6, with the same advantage to the bank. Odds of 15 *for* 1 are offered for 3 and 11, the advantage still being 16·667 per cent. All craps are offered at 8 *for* 1, an advantage to the bank of 11·111 per cent.

Free or Odds Bets. When the shooter has a point, casinos allow players who have bet on pass, don't pass, come or don't come to double their bets, and the second half of the bet is paid at the correct odds. Thus pass or come bettors will get 2−1 on points 4 and 10, don't pass or don't come bettors will get 1−2. The odds offered on 5 and 9 will be 3−2 and 2−3 respectively, and on 6 and 8, 6−5 and 5−6. For example, a come bettor with a point of 6 and a stake of five chips will be allowed a free or odds bet of five chips on 6, to be paid at odds of 6−5. As the casino will not deal in fractions of a chip, the stake on this particular free bet must always be in multiples of five, and the player will be allowed to round up or down his stake to the nearest multiple of five. If his stake is only one or two chips he will not be allowed a free bet at all. The casino allows the free bet to speed up the action, and takes no commission on it. Thus the player should always accept it for the maximum stake allowed, and correspondingly reduce the bank's advantage on the total bet. Free bet stakes are not placed flat on the table, but overlap the edge of the original stake.

The bank's overall advantage on the bet can be calculated by reference to Table 1. Of the 1980 rolls summarized, the bank returns to the pass line bettor 976×2 chips (assuming one chip per bet), or 1952 chips. The table shows that 1320 of the 1980 rolls will result in a point and if the pass bettor takes the free bet each time he will stake a further 1320 chips, and, since the bets are paid at the correct odds, can expect 1320 chips back in return. Thus, if he always accepts the free bets, his total stakes on the 1980 rolls will be $1980 + 1320$, or 3300 chips, from which in the long run he will expect $1952 + 1320$ back, or 3272. So he will expect to lose only 28 chips in 3300, a casino advantage of only 0·848 per cent. Don't pass bettors will do even better, with an advantage to the bank of only 0·832 per cent. This is the lowest advantage the casino takes in crap games, except for some casinos in Reno, where free bets are allowed of double the original stake. A player making full use of these bets will reduce the casino's advantage to 0·606 per cent on pass or come bets and 0·595 per cent on don't pass or don't come bets.

Private Craps
Craps played privately is a much simpler game than casino craps. The only essential equipment is a pair of dice, although a blanket or carpet might be used to roll them on, and a backboard for the dice to rebound from is advisable. Because of the lack of a staking table, the bets are fewer and simpler.

The first shooter places a sum of money before him as his 'centre' bet, and the other players are invited to 'fade' it. The shooter is betting he will win; the other players put up an amount equal to his stake to bet he will lose. It is an even money bet. As in the casino game, the shooter wins if he throws a natural 7 or 11, loses if he throws a crap 2, 3 or 12, and continues to roll if he establishes a point.

Meanwhile, the other players bet among themselves on whether the shooter passes or not. Come and don't come bets are also made. Once a shooter has thrown his point, he and other players may bet that he will or will not make it. The correct odds are paid, i.e. 6—5 that he will make 6 or 8, 3—2 that he will make 5 or 9, and 2—1 that he will make 4 or 10. Sometimes even money is bet on the shooter making a point of 6 or 8, but this is incorrect, and gives the wrong bettor a tremendous advantage. Hardway bets are common. If the shooter's point is 4 or 10, 8—1 are the odds against making it the hard way. It is 10—1 against making a hardway 6 or 8. The players may make other bets among themselves, but those already mentioned are the commonest.

The shooter keeps the dice while winning; as soon as he misses out he passes the dice to the next player in rotation.

Strategy
Craps is a game of chance, and skilful play consists only of knowing the proper odds and probabilities for each bet, and making bets which are arithmetically sound. In private crap games the wrong bettor generally has an advantage of 1·414 per cent, a significant advantage over a long period. In casino games, a sound bet is merely one with a small advantage to the casino. The player will therefore avoid, for example, Big Six, Big Eight and hardway bets. Wrong bettors face a slightly smaller disadvantage than right bettors. If the free or odds bets are made whenever possible, the casino's advantage can be kept below 1 per cent.